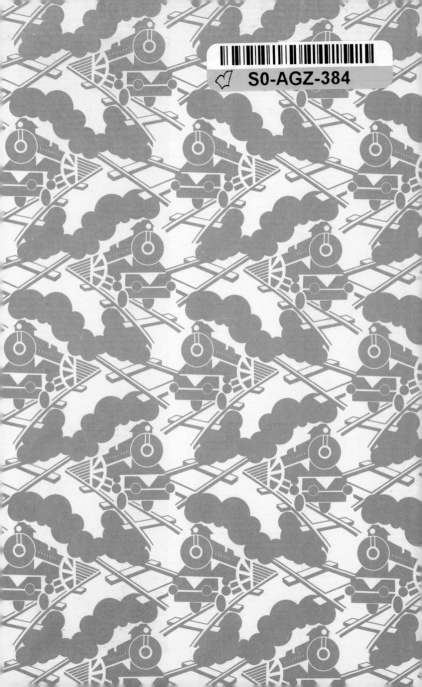

THE RAILWAY BOOK

"Romance!" the season-tickets mourn,
    "*He* never ran to catch his train,
But passed with coach and guard and horn—
    And left the local—late again!"
Confound Romance! . . . And all unseen
Romance brought up the nine-fifteen.

RUDYARD KIPLING

The Railway Book

AN ANTHOLOGY

EDITED BY

STUART LEGG

FOURTH ESTATE

LONDON

First published in Great Britain in 1952
This edition first published in Great Britain in 1988 by
Fourth Estate Limited
113 Westbourne Grove
London W2 4UP

Copyright in this selection © 1988 by Stuart Legg
Preface copyright © 1988 by Miles Kington

British Library Cataloguing in Publication Data

The railway book.—2nd ed.
  1. English literature, to 1981. Special
  subjects: Railways – Anthologies
  I. Legg, Stuart
  820.8'0356

  ISBN 0-947795-08-1

Printed and bound in Great Britain by
WBC Print Ltd, Bristol.

Contents

NEWCASTLE

AND

CARLISLE

Railway.

Notice is hereby Given,

THAT all Persons trespassing on the Railway, or the Works thereof, are liable *to a considerable Penalty* for each Offence. And that the Punishment for doing any Injury or Damage to the said Railway is

Transportation for 7 Years.

THE DIRECTORS GIVE THIS PUBLIC

WARNING,

that they are determined to Prosecute with the utmost Rigour, all Persons who may do any such Injury or Damage to the Railway; and that positive Orders are given to all the Servants of the Company, to give Information against any Persons trespassing thereon.

JOHN ADAMSON,
Clerk to the Company.

Railway Office, Newcastle upon Tyne,
21st August, 1835

Preface

This is my kind of book. It is my kind of book not only because I enjoyed discovering it hugely, but because it is the kind of book I want to do myself. In fact, it is the kind of book I am going to do myself. In fact, I would go so far as to say that it is the kind of book that every railway lover is going to do some day.

As a part explanation for this strange statement, I would like to call Ludovic Kennedy as witness. He did a good anthology of train writing some years back, and followed it up with an anthology on boats and another one on planes, all excellent. But he confessed to me last year when I asked him about it that the railway book had sold much better than the others, though he could not think why.

'Are railway people more literate than other people?' he wanted to know. 'Do they have more spare time for reading? Are there more of them? Are they more nostalgic?'

No, Mr Kennedy. I think the answer is that they are more jealous. Every railway lover, I am convinced, has the makings of a book in him which he does not even confess to himself. I, for instance, read twenty years ago a thrilling account by the French writer Theophile Gautier of the first trains in France to travel at speed, and I thought to myself at the time: I must make a note of this, because it has never been translated into English and may come in useful. I later came across a humorous piece by another French writer, Alphonse Allais, in which he suggested that railways could maximise their profits by erecting large hoardings at the side of the rail on which were written, in huge print, the latest novels. Passengers would travel from Marseille to Paris staring out of the window and reading at the same time—and the novel would have got to a very exciting bit when they arrived in Paris, so they would have to buy a further ticket on to Le Havre just to see what happened.

Other bits and pieces of railway oddities like this I have stored over the years. I now realise why. Deep down, I am planning my own railway anthology. And so is everyone else.

In the mid-1980s I had the luck to find myself involved in a BBC film about the Duchess of Hamilton, the venerable steam engine which operated out of York. One day they took her on a special outing over the Settle-Carlisle line, one of those outings which is accompanied by thousands of men with serious looks and cameras, or orange jackets and dirty hands, depending on whether they had come to look or help. And I suddenly realised that almost everyone there, including me, was making their own film, or TV programme, or documentary, or dossier. I said as much to one of the orange-jacketed operatives, one of the very few who was content to just wield a spade.

'Actually,' he said, 'I've already written a book. About the Duchess of Hamilton. Do you want to buy a copy?'

He didn't show any signs of wanting to do another train book. Perhaps, once the ideal has been achieved, the passion dies away. Ludovic Kennedy has not done another train book. And nor has Stuart Legg, so far as I know, since he edited this cornucopia in 1952. In Legg's case, I am not at all surprised—he seems to have got all the best stuff in already. The long letter from Sydney Smith on p 95 is worth the price of admission alone, and reading through the rest, whether it is T. E. Lawrence on blowing up trains or the Countess of Zetland on nearly being burnt alive in one while sitting in her carriage, I realise that I am condemned to making do with the second-rate for my book.

Not quite, perhaps. I once came across a wonderful autobiography of a Victorian railway porter which Mr Legg has not plundered. (The porter relates that at Paddington everyone's luggage was stored under the letter with which the passenger's name began, A for Allan and so on. The porter was mystified once at being reported for swearing at a passenger who had asked after his luggage. The passenger was Mr Lambert, and what the porter had said to him was: "Go to L".) When I was literary editor at *Punch* I had a reissue of this autobiography reviewed by the individualistic Mr Gerard Fiennes—which reminds me, that there is a very fine radio broadcast in the archives of the BBC by Mr Fiennes entitled 'Sex and the railways', which I would also like to have in my anthology. . .

Put it this way. This book is unquestionably the finest railway anthology and scrapbook—until mine appears.

MILES KINGTON

Limpley Stoke, 1988

Introduction

You could call this a collection of corner-seat reading. As such, it is intended to appeal to everyone—to everyone, that is, who regards a train journey as more than a tiresome interval between two places. And lest it be held that the savouring of smoke and steam is essentially a male pastime, I should say at once that the idea of putting it together came from a woman. Miss Janet Adam Smith suggested this book; to her, therefore, and to my other two lively collaborators, Rupert Hart-Davis and Richard Garnett, will justly go the credit for the pleasure it may give.

To me, since for some reason my name alone has filtered on to the cover, will go any corresponding degree of blame. It will therefore be both seemly and wise for me to temper with suitable humility our sweeping claim to appeal to everyone. For it is possible that "everyone" may include members of that distinguished and vigilant fraternity—pillars of the church, of the academic world, of the professions, of the Upper Sixth—who are railway experts. In railway society, knowledge runs profound and feeling high; in railway fanaticism, rival loves and hates recognize few bounds; in railway disputation, hair-splitting can be medieval in its nicety. Woe, in this implacable company, to the unwary partisan; woe, woe, to the inaccurate. To the refuge of humility, without delay.

Our sole aim here has been to capture something of the tang and flavour of the writing produced by the impact of railways on affairs and literature. And in so aiming, we have sought only to interest and amuse. True, among the lineside observations of monarchs and statesmen, travellers and journalists, novelists and poets, we have included many descriptions of railway occasions which in themselves evoke affection or command remark. But we could not hope, and have not tried, to give any proportionate picture of

10

railway development in so short a book. Frequently, it is the very size of the original canvas that prohibits the adequate selection of details from it. Sir Francis Head's eyewitness account, for instance, of the scene at the Menai Strait when the tubes of the Britannia Bridge were floated, occupies many pages; and to condense it would be to lose at once the vivid, panoramic majesty of the moment he presents. A similar scale of space is needed to convey, from the contemporary reports, any sense of the miracle of enduring human will that went into the building of the early lines with implements which were virtually those of a previous agricultural age; of the complex and ingenious methods of fraud that sometimes accompanied their financing; of the protracted controversies—like the Battle of the Gauges—that shook the committee-rooms of Westminster, and so on. The railway historians of the nineteenth century approached their grand themes on a grand scale: to deny the scale would often be to rob their work of its own grandeur— and perhaps worse, of its grandiosity.

Nor could we, for reasons of expense as well as space, make any pretence at completeness when it came to extracting from the references to railways made by the imaginative writers. Kipling, for example, will prove rewarding to those who wish to range this fascinating field beyond our rigid limits. He wrote a short story round an engine; in *The Jungle Book* he reflected the Mugger's dim views of the Delhi Mail; and many of his other works are likewise dotted with railway incident and imagery. Conan Doyle's splendid tale *The Lost Special* marks the beginning of that long tradition of detective fiction which has so fruitfully used railways as the instruments of crime—a tradition which frequently matures today in the books of, among others, Mr. Michael Innes and Mr. Freeman Wills Crofts. The short excerpts we have included from *The Octopus* by Frank Norris and *La Bête Humaine* by Émile Zola will serve as samples of at least two full-length novels whose plots are woven round the permanent way. And if I may be allowed to digress briefly into my own field of films, I would recommend that no seeker after railway thrills should miss a revival of that classic of the silent screen, *The General*. In it, for a whole gorgeous hour and more, Buster Keaton and a locomotive explore

to the frontiers of the possible every perversion of sane practice
which might feature in the nightmares of a Superintendent of the
Line.

It only remains for me to indicate that the sources of the passages
included will be found in the notes at the end of the book; and to
thank my collaborators both for their hard work in assembling
the mass of material available for any anthology of railway writing,
and for their endless patience and good humour through the
laborious hours of its sifting, editing and ordering.

We hope that you will now enjoy the ride as much as we
enjoyed marshalling the train.

STUART LEGG

Farnham, 1952

For permission to reprint copyright passages my gratitude is due
to: the Editors of The Times (Note No. 100); The Sunday Times
(No. 107); New Statesman (No. 116); Jonathan Cape Ltd (Nos. 61,
113, 114); William Collins, Sons & Co. Ltd. (No. 96); Constable &
Co. Ltd. (No. 36); Duckworth & Co. Ltd. (No. 98); Faber & Faber
(Nos. 126, 129); Michael Innes, Victor Gollancz Ltd. (Nos. 123,
130); David Higham Associates Ltd. (No. 146); Longman Group
UK Ltd. (No. 22); Methuen Ltd. (No. 106); A D Peters & Co. Ltd.
(No. 131); Mr George Sassoon (No. 94); Richard Scott Simon Ltd.
(No. 149); Secker & Warburg Ltd. (Nos. 95, 115); Unwin Hyman
Ltd. (Nos. 88 etc.).

The Ringing Grooves of Change

TREVITHICKS,
PORTABLE STEAM ENGINE,

Catch me who can.

Mechanical Power Subduing
Animal Speed.

1. OPENING OF THE MERTHYR TYDVIL, 1804

QUAINT, rattling, puffing, asthmatic, and wheezy, the pioneer of ten thousand gilding creations of beauty and strength made its way between the whitewashed houses of the old tramway at Merthyr. It had a dwarf body placed on a high framework, constructed by the hedge carpenter of the place in the roughest possible fashion. The wheels were equally rough and large, and surmounting all was a huge stack, ugly enough when it was new, but in after times made uglier by whitewash and rust. Every movement was made with a hideous uproar, snorting and clanking, and this, aided by the noise of the escaping steam, formed a tableau from which, met in the byeway, every old woman would run with affright. . . . Great was the concourse assembled: villagers of all ages and sizes thronged the spot; and the rumour of the day's doings even penetrated up the defiles of Taff Vawr and Taff Vach, bringing down old apple-faced farmers and their wives, who were told of a power and a speed that would alter everything, and do away with horses altogether. Prim, cosy, apple-faced people, innocent and primitive, little thought ye then of the changes which the clanking monster was to yield; how Grey Dobbin would see flying by a mass of wood and iron, thousands of tons of weight, bearing not only the commerce of the country, but hundreds of people as well; how rivers and mountains would afford no obstacle, as the mighty azure waves leap the one and dash through the other. . . . The driver was one William Richards, and on the engine were perched Trevithick and Rees Jones, their faces black, but their eyes bright with the anticipation of victory. Soon the signal was given, and amidst a mighty roar from the people, the wheels turned and the mass moved forward, going steadily at the rate of five miles an hour until a bridge was reached a little below the town that did not admit of the stack going under, and as this was built of bricks, there was a great crash and instant stoppage. Trevithick and Jones were of the old-fashioned school of men who did not believe in impossibilities. The fickle crowd, too, who had hurrahed like mad, hung back and said, "It won't do"; but these heroes, the advance-guard of a race who had done more to make England famous than battles by land or sea, sprang to the ground and worked like Britons, never ceasing until they had repaired the mishap, and then they rattled on, and finally reached their journey's end.

THE WESTERN MAIL

2. THE RAIN-HILL TRIALS, 1829

On Tuesday, the first day of trial, the race-ground presented a scene of extraordinary gaiety and bustle. The day being remarkably fine, thousands of persons of all ranks were assembled from the surrounding towns and districts. Upwards of 10,000 persons were computed to have been present, among whom were a greater number of scientific men, and practical engineers, than have been assembled on any previous occasion. The ground was extremely favourable for the spectators, and the performances of the different carriages were such as to excite the strongest feelings of admiration and surprise.

During the whole of the day the different carriages were exhibiting on the Rail-Way, and it is scarcely possible for any one who has not seen them in motion to form any conception of their astonishing speed. In the early part of the day, the carriage of Mr. Robert Stephenson, of Newcastle, attracted great attention. It ran, without any weight attached to it, at the rate of 24 miles in the hour, rushing past the spectators with amazing velocity. It has been stated by several of the papers that it emitted very little smoke; but the fact is, that during the trial it emitted none. Previous to the trial, a little coal was put into it, and then it sent forth a smoke; but after the trial had commenced, it used coke, which, as it does not produce any smoke, of course could not emit any. We know that there were some persons on the ground who mistook steam for smoke.

Mr. Hackworth, of Darlington, ran his carriage along the course during the day; but no trial of its speed with weights took place.

Mr. Winan's machine, worked by two men, and carrying six passengers, was also on the ground. It moved with no great velocity compared to the Locomotive Steam-Carriages, but with considerable speed considering that it was put in motion by human power. One of its wheels was damaged in the course of the afternoon, by Mr. Hackworth's Locomotive Steam-Carriage.

Mr. Brandreth's horse-power Locomotive Engine exhibited, not in the way of competition, but as exercise. About fifty persons clung round the waggons, giving a gross weight, with the machine, of about 5 tons, and with this weight, the horses (themselves moving scarcely one mile and a quarter an hour) propelled the waggons and load exactly at the rate of five miles an hour.

The engine of Messrs. Braithwaite and Erickson, of London, was universally allowed to exhibit, in appearance and compactness, the beau-ideal of a Locomotive Carriage. Its performance, whilst exercising without a load, was most astonishing, passing over a space of $2\frac{3}{4}$ miles in seven minutes and a quarter, including a stoppage; it actually did one mile in the incredibly short space of one minute and thirty-three seconds! The velocity with which the Novelty moved, surprized and amazed every beholder. It seemed indeed to fly, presenting one of the most sublime spectacles of mechanical ingenuity and human daring the world ever beheld. It actually made one giddy to look at it, and filled the breasts of thousands with lively fears for the safety of the individuals who were on it, and who seemed not to run along the earth, but to fly, as it were, "on the wings of the wind."

The preliminaries of weighing, &c. being concluded, the Novelty, with her appointed load, started, and performed the first trip of three miles and a half in good style. On the second journey, however, owing to an accident to one of the pipes, all locomotion was suspended; and before the injury, though unimportant, could be repaired, the day was too far advanced to recommence her allotted task. It was evident, from the frequent though slight, derangements which had occurred to this engine, that a little further time was desirable before her performance should be again brought under the special notice of the judges. On the Saturday afternoon, however, the injury sustained being repaired, she appeared again on the course, with the Directors' carriage attached to her, in which were about forty ladies and gentlemen, and with which she moved along in beautiful style at the almost incredible speed of upwards of 30 miles per hour! In the course of the day, Mr. Stephenson's engine also performed an equally brilliant feat. Between the occurrence and the repair of the accident to Messrs. Braithwaite's carriage, that of Mr. Stephenson's, the Rocket, ran, without load or tender, 7 miles in 14 minutes, which is at the rate of 30 miles an hour; and one of the trips of $3\frac{1}{2}$ miles was performed in 6 minutes and 37 seconds, which is at the rate of 32 miles an hour!

THE LIVERPOOL TIMES, 13 October 1829

3. THE LOCO MOTIVE MACHINE

Nov. 14th, 1829—Today we have had a *lark* of a very high order. Lady Wilton sent over yesterday from Knowsley to say that the Loco Motive machine was to be upon the railway at such a place at 12 o'clock for the Knowsley party to ride in if they liked, and inviting this house to be of the party. So of course we were at our post in 3 carriages and some horsemen at the hour appointed. I had the satisfaction, for I can't call it *pleasure*, of taking a trip of five miles in it, which we did in just a quarter of an hour—that is, 20 miles an hour. As accuracy upon this subject was my great object, I held my watch in my hand at starting, and all the time; and as it has a second hand, I knew I could not be deceived; and so it turned out there was not the difference of a second between the coachee or conductor and myself. But observe, during these five miles, the machine was occasionally made to put itself out or *go it*; and then we went at the rate of 23 miles an hour, and just with the same ease as to motion or absence of friction as the other reduced pace. But the quickest motion is to me *frightful*: it is really flying, and it is impossible to divest yourself of the notion of instant death to all upon the least accident happening. It gave me a headache which has not left me yet. Sefton is convinced that some damnable thing must come of it; but he and I seem more struck with such apprehension than others. . . . The smoke is very inconsiderable indeed, but sparks of fire are abroad in some quantity: one burnt Miss de Ros's cheek, another a hole in Lady Maria's silk pelisse, and a third a hole in someone else's gown. Altogether I am extremely glad indeed to have seen this miracle, and to have travelled in it. Had I thought worse of it than I do, I should have had the curiosity to try it; but, having done so, I am quite satisfied with my *first* achievement being my *last*.

THOMAS CREEVEY

4. A FOOTPLATE RUN WITH STEPHENSON

Liverpool, *August* [26th 1830]

My dear H.,

A common sheet of paper is enough for love, but a foolscap extra can alone contain a railroad and my ecstasies. . . . We were introduced to the little engine which was to drag us along the rails. She (for they make these curious little fire-horses all mares) consisted of a boiler, a stove, a small platform—a bench, and behind the bench a barrel, containing enough water to prevent her being thirsty for fifteen miles—the whole not bigger than a common fire-engine. She goes upon ten wheels which are her feet, and are moved by bright steel legs called pistons; these are propelled by steam, and in proportion as more steam is applied to the upper extremities

(the hip-joints I suppose) of these pistons, the faster they
move the wheels; and when it is desirable to diminish the
speed, the steam, which unless suffered to escape would burst
the boiler, evaporates through a safety-valve into the air. The
reins, bit, and bridle of this wonderful beast is a small steel
handle, which applies or withdraws the steam from the legs
or pistons, so that a child might manage it. The coals, which
are its oats, were under the bench, and there was a small glass
tube affixed to the boiler, with water in it, which indicates by
its fulness or emptiness when the creature wants water, which
is immediately conveyed to it from its reservoirs. There is a
chimney to the stove; but, as they burn coke, there is none of
the dreadful black smoke which accompanies the progress
of a steam-vessel. This snorting little animal, which I felt
rather inclined to pat, was then harnessed to our carriage,
and, Mr. Stephenson having taken me on the bench of the
engine with him, we started at about ten miles an hour. . . .

You can't imagine how strange it seemed to be journeying
on thus, without any visible cause of progress other than the
magical machine, with the flying white breath and rhythmical
unvarying pace, between these rocky walls, which are already
clothed with moss, and ferns, and grasses; and, when I
reflected that these great masses of stone had been cut asunder
to allow our passage thus far below the surface of the earth,
I felt as if no fairy tale was ever half so wonderful as what
I saw. Bridges were thrown from side to side across the top
of these cliffs, and the people looking down upon us from
them seemed like pigmies standing in the sky. I must be more
concise though, or I shall want room. . . . We had now come
fifteen miles, and stopped where the road traversed a wide
and deep valley. Stephenson made me alight, and led me
down to the bottom of this ravine, over which, in order to
keep his road level, he has thrown a magnificent viaduct of
nine arches, one of which is 70 feet high, through which we

saw the whole of this beautiful little valley. It was lovely and wonderful beyond all words. . . . He explained to me the whole construction of the steam-engine, and said he could soon make a famous engineer of me, which, considering the wonderful things he *has* achieved, I dare not say is impossible. His way of explaining himself is peculiar, but very striking, and I understood without difficulty all that he said to me.

We then rejoined the rest of the party, and, the engine having received its supply of water, the carriage was placed behind it, for it cannot turn, and was set off at its utmost speed, thirty-five miles an hour; swifter than a bird flies (for they tried the experiment with a snipe). You cannot conceive what that sensation of cutting the air was; the motion is as smooth as possible too. I could either have read or written; and, as it was, I stood up and with my bonnet off " drank the air before me." . . . When I closed my eyes, this sensation of flying was quite delightful, and strange beyond description; yet, strange as it was, I had a perfect sense of security and not the slightest fear. At one time, to exhibit the power of the engine, having met another steam carriage, which was un-supplied with water, Mr. Stephenson caused it to be fastened in front of ours; moreover a wagon laden with timber was also chained to us, and thus propelling the idle steam-engine, and dragging the loaded wagon which was beside it, and our own carriage full of people behind, this brave little she-dragon of ours flew on. Further on she met three carts, which being fastened in front of her, she pushed on before her without the slightest delay or difficulty. When I add that this pretty little creature can run with equal facility either backwards or forwards, I believe I have given you an account of all her capacities.

Now for a word or two about the master of these marvels. with whom I am horribly in love. He is a man of from fifty to fifty-five years of age; his face is fine though careworn, and bears an expression of deep thoughtfulness; his mode of explaining his ideas is peculiar and very original, striking, and forcible; and although his accent indicates strongly his north-country birth, his language has not the slightest touch of vulgarity or coarseness. He has certainly turned my head.

FRANCES ANNE KEMBLE

5. THE LIVERPOOL & MANCHESTER

JUNE 9th, 1833 (Liverpool). At twelve I got upon an omnibus, and was driven up a steep hill to the place where the steam-carriages start. We travelled in the second class of carriages. There were five carriages linked together, in each of which were placed open seats for the traveller, four and four facing each other; but not all were full; and, besides, there was a close carriage, and also a machine for luggage. The fare was four shillings for the thirty-one miles. Everything went on so rapidly, that I had scarcely the power of observation. The road begins at an excavation through rock, and is to a certain extent insulated from the adjacent country. It is occasionally placed on bridges, and frequently intersected by ordinary roads. Not quite a perfect level is preserved. On setting out there is a slight jolt, arising from the chain catching each carriage, but, once in motion, we proceeded as smoothly as possible. For a minute or two the pace is gentle, and is constantly varying. The machine produces little smoke or steam. First in order is the tall chimney; then the boiler, a barrel-like vessel; than an oblong reservoir of water; then a vehicle for coals; and then comes, of a length infinitely extendible, the train of carriages. If all the seats had been filled, our train would have carried about 150 passengers; but a gentleman assured me at Chester that he went with a thousand persons to Newton fair. There must have been two engines then.

I have heard since that two thousand persons and more went to and from the fair that day. But two thousand only, at three shillings each way, would have produced £600! But, after all, the expense is so great, that it is considered uncertain whether the establishment will ultimately remunerate the proprietors. Yet I have heard that it already yields the shareholders a dividend of nine per cent. . . .

I should have observed before that the most remarkable movements of the journey are those in which trains pass one another. The rapidity is such that there is no recognizing the features of a traveller. On several occasions, the noise of the passing engine was like the whizzing of a rocket. Guards are stationed in the road, holding flags, giving notice to the drivers when to stop. Near Newton, I noticed an inscription recording the memorable death of Huskisson.[1]

CRABB ROBINSON

6. NOTHING MORE COMFORTABLE

KNOWSLEY, July 18th [1837]. Tired of doing nothing in London, and of hearing about the Queen, and the elections, I resolved to vary the scene and run down here to see the Birmingham railroad, Liverpool, and Liverpool races. So I started at five o'clock on Sunday evening, got to Birmingham at half-past five on Monday morning, and got upon the railroad at half-past seven. Nothing can be more comfortable than the vehicle in which I was put, a sort of chariot with two places, and there is nothing disagreeable about it but the occasional whiffs of stinking air which it is impossible to exclude altogether. The first sensation is a slight degree of nervousness and a feeling of being run away with, but a sense of security soon supervenes, and the velocity is delightful. Town after

[1] See page 90.

town, one park and *château* after another are left behind with the rapid variety of a moving panorama, and the continual bustle and animation of the changes and stoppages make the journey very entertaining. The train was very long, and heads were continually popping out of the several carriages, attracted by well-known voices, and then came the greetings and exclamations of surprise, the "Where are you going?" and "How on earth came you here?" Considering the novelty of its establishment, there is very little embarrassment, and it certainly renders all other travelling irksome and tedious by comparison. It was peculiarly gay at this time, because there was so much going on. There were all sorts of people going to Liverpool races, barristers to the assizes, and candidates to their several elections.

CHARLES GREVILLE

7. PARLIAMENTARY COMMITTEE

WHEN I went to Liverpool to plan a line from thence to Manchester, I pledged myself to the directors to attain a speed of ten miles an hour. I said I had no doubt the locomotive might be made to go much faster, but that we had better be moderate at the beginning. The directors said I was quite right; for that if, when they went to Parliament, I talked of going at a greater rate than ten miles an hour, I should put a cross upon the concern. It was not an easy task for me to keep the engine down to ten miles an hour, but it must be done, and I did my best. I had to place myself in that most unpleasant of all positions—the witness-box of a Parliamentary Committee. I was not long in it, before I began to wish for a hole to creep out at. I could not find words to satisfy either the Committee or myself. I was subjected to the cross-examination of eight or ten barristers, purposely, as far as possible, to bewilder me. Some member of the Committee asked if I was a foreigner, and another hinted that I was mad.

MR. GEORGE STEPHENSON

I SAY he never had a plan; I do not believe he is capable of making one. His is a mind perpetually fluctuating between opposite difficulties; he neither knows whether he is to make bridges over roads or rivers; or of one size or another; or to make embankments, or cuttings, or inclined planes, or in what way the thing is to be carried into effect. Whenever a difficulty is pressed, as in the case of the tunnels, he gets out of it at one end; and when you try to catch him there, he gets out at the other.

MR. ALDERSON (against the Bill)

NONE of the tremendous consequences have ensued from the use of steam in land carriage that have been stated. The horses have not started, nor the cows ceased to give their milk, nor have ladies miscarried at the sight of these things going forward at the rate of four miles and a half an hour.

MR. JOY (for the Bill)

8. LANDOWNERS v. SURVEYORS

THE duties of the surveyor were not free from danger. The landed proprietor often refused admission to the trespasser and to his theodolite. At Addington the surveyors were met and defied in such force, that after a brief fight they were secured, carried before a magistrate, and fined. At Saxby, when they were ordered off, they produced pistols in defence, but after a general scuffle were lodged in the county-gaol. Near Osberton they were treated as poachers, and only escaped the penalty from their imposing numbers. Dukes perilled the honour of their escutcheons in open fights with the general enemy. Fines were frequent, and constables were at a premium. At Lincoln, fraud was found better than force; and while a crafty surveyor endeavoured to persuade a refractory landowner, his coadjutors were calmly performing their work. In Oxfordshire a fierce warfare arose, nor could the survey be continued until after a severe conflict, and under the care of a body of armed men.

The engineers were in truth driven to adopt whatever method might occur to them. While the people were at church; while the villager took his rustic meal; with dark lanthorns during the dark hours; by force, by fraud, by any and every mode they could devise, they carried the object which they felt to be necessary but knew to be wrong. Such was another phase of the morality of the rail.

JOHN FRANCIS

9. SURVEYORS *v.* LANDOWNERS

"LANDOWNERS," wrote *Fraser's Magazine*, "were kept in a constant state of anxiety by rumours of the course each railway was likely to pursue. Young gentlemen with theodolites and chains marched about the fields; long white sticks with bits of paper attached were carried ruthlessly through fields, gardens, and sometimes even through houses." Colonel Sibthorpe said, "The injuries done by the engineers of railway companies to the property of private individuals was most unjust. Not content with making encroachments in the daytime, these marauders of engineers took advantage of the darkness to commit those trespasses which their modesty would not suffer them to do at another time. An honourable friend of his rose one morning and actually found a flag stuck up before his very door." There can be no doubt that the insolent assurance of many connected with railroads was unbounded. One proprietor, when he asked the promoters what would be given him for the land which a line was to traverse, was informed "they would tell him when the bill was passed into a law. That they did not care whether he consented or not; that the railway department of the board of trade had already reported in favour of the line, and it would be the worse for him if he offered opposition." Another was told that if he objected to the rail passing near his lawn, it would be taken through his kitchen. Ladies of title were impudently assured that they must get used to railways as others had done.

JOHN FRANCIS

10. THE SHAREHOLDERS

HERE are the shareholders diffused throughout the whole kingdom in towns and country houses, knowing nothing of each other, and too remote to co-operate were they acquainted. Very few of them see a railway journal; not many a daily one; and scarcely any know much of railway politics. Necessarily a fluctuating body, only a small number are familiar with the Company's history—its acts, engagements, policy, management. A great proportion are incompetent to judge of the questions that come before them, and lack decision to act out such judgments as they may form—executors who do not like to take steps involving much responsibility; trustees fearful of interfering with the property under their care, lest possible loss should entail a lawsuit; widows who have never in their lives acted for themselves in any affair of moment; maiden ladies, alike nervous and innocent of all business knowledge; clergymen whose daily discipline has been little calculated to make them acute men of the world; retired trades-men whose retail transactions have given them small ability for grasping large considerations; servants possessed of accumulated savings and cramped notions; with sundry others of like helpless character—all of them rendered more or less conservative by ignorance or timidity, and proportionately inclined to support those in authority. Turn now to those whose efforts are directed to railway expansion. Consider the constant pressure of local interests—of small towns, of rural districts, of landowners—all of them eager for branch accommodation; all of them with great and definite advantages in view; few of them conscious of the loss those advantages may entail on others. Remember the influence of legislators, prompted some by their constituents, some by personal aims, and encouraged, most of them, by the belief that additional railway facilities are in every case nationally beneficial; and then calculate the extent to which, as stated to Mr. Card-well's Committee, Parliament has "excited and urged forward" Companies into rivalry. Observe the temptations under which lawyers are placed—the vast profits accruing to them from every railway contest, whether ending in success or failure; and then imagine the magnitude and subtlety of their extension manœuvring. Conceive the urgency of the engineering profession, to the richer of whom more railway-making means more wealth; to the mass of whom more railway-making means daily bread. Estimate the capitalist-power of contractors, whose unemployed plant brings heavy loss; whose plant when employed brings great gain. Then recollect that to these last—lawyers, engineers, and contractors—the getting up and executing of new undertakings is a business—a business to which every energy is directed; in which long years of practice have given great skill; and to the facilitation of which all means tolerated by men of the world are thought justifiable. Finally, consider that the classes inter-ested in carrying out new schemes are in constant communi-cation, and have every facility for combined action. A great part of them live in London, and most of these have offices at Westminster—in Great George Street, in Parliament

Street, clustering round the Legislature. Not only are they
thus concentrated, not only are they throughout the year in
frequent business intercourse, but during the session they are
daily together, in Palace Yard hotels, in the lobbies, in the
committee-rooms, in the House of Commons itself. Is it any
wonder then that the wide-spread, ill-formed, unorganised
body of shareholders standing severally alone, and each preoccupied with his daily affairs, should be continually out-
generalled by the comparatively small but active, skilful,
combined body opposed to them, whose very occupation is at
stake in gaining the victory?

HERBERT SPENCER

11. BRUNEL'S ALARM CLOCK

[Brilliant and unorthodox, Isambard Kingdom Brunel was
one of the giants of the nineteenth-century engineering scene.
Always overworked, he was a heavy smoker; wherever he
went, his immense leather cigar-case, holding fifty cigars,
went with him. In 1833, at the age of 26, he was appointed
Engineer to the Great Western Railway Company, then
about to begin the building of its main line from London to
Bristol.]

IN 1833 Brunel and I occupied chambers facing each other in
Parliament Street, and as my duties involved the superinten-
dence, as Parliamentary agent, of the compliance with all the
Standing Orders of Parliament, and very frequent interviews
and negotiations with the landowners on the line, we were of
necessity constantly thrown together. To facilitate our intercourse, it occurred to Brunel to carry a string across Parliament Street, from his chambers to mine, to be there connected with a bell, by which he could either call me to the
window to receive his telegraphic signals, or, more frequently, to wake me up in the morning when we had occasion

to go into the country together, which, it is needless to observe, was of frequent occurrence; and great was the astonishment of the neighbours at this device, the object of which they were unable to comprehend.

I believe that at that time he scarcely ever went to bed, though I never remember to have seen him tired or out of spirits. He was a very constant smoker, and would take his nap in an armchair, very frequently with a cigar in his mouth; and if we were to start out of town at five or six o'clock in the morning, it was his frequent practice to rouse me out of bed about three, by means of the bell, when I would invariably find him up and dressed, and in great glee at the fun of having curtailed my slumbers by two or three hours more than necessary.

ST. GEORGE BURKE, Q.C.

12. THE CAMDEN TOWN CUTTING

THE first shock of a great earthquake had, just at the period, rent the whole neighbourhood to its centre. Traces of its course were visible on every side. Houses were knocked down; streets broken through and stopped; deep pits and trenches dug in the ground; enormous heaps of earth and clay thrown up; buildings that were undermined and shaking, propped by great beams of wood. Here, a chaos of carts, overthrown and jumbled together, lay topsy-turvy at the bottom of a steep, unnatural hill; there, confused treasures of iron soaked and rusted in something that had accidentally become a pond. Everywhere were bridges that led nowhere; thoroughfares that were wholly impassable; Babel towers of chimneys, wanting half their height; temporary wooden houses and enclosures, in the most unlikely situations; carcasses of ragged tenements, and fragments of unfinished walls and arches, and piles of scaffolding and wildernesses of bricks, and giant forms of cranes, and tripods straddling above nothing. There were a hundred thousand shapes and substances of incompleteness, wildly mingled out of their places, upside down, burrowing in the earth, aspiring in the air, mouldering in the water, and unintelligible as any dream. Hot springs and fiery eruptions, the usual attendants upon earthquakes, lent their contributions of confusion to the scene. Boiling water hissed and heaved within dilapidated walls, whence, also, the glare and roar of flames came issuing forth; and mounds of ashes blocked up rights of way, and wholly changed the law and custom of the neighbourhood.

In short, the yet unfinished and unopened railroad was in progress; and, from the very core of all this dire disorder, tailed smoothly away upon its mighty course of civilization and improvement.

But, as yet, the neighbourhood was shy to own the railroad. One or two bold speculators had projected streets; and one had built a little, but had stopped among the mud and ashes to consider further of it. A brand-new tavern, redolent of fresh mortar and size, and fronting nothing at all, had taken for its sign The Railway Arms; but that might be rash enterprise—and then it hoped to sell drink to the workmen. So, the Excavators' House of Call had sprung up from a beershop: and the old-established ham and beef shop had become the Railway Eating House, with a roast leg of pork daily, through interested motives of a similar immediate and popular description. Lodging-house keepers were favourable in like manner, and for the like reasons were not to be trusted. The general belief was very slow. There were frowzy fields, and cow-houses, and dunghills, and dustheaps, and ditches, and gardens, and summer-houses, and carpet-beating grounds, at the very door of the railway. Little tumuli of oyster shells in the oyster season, and of lobster shells in the lobster season, and of broken crockery and faded cabbage leaves in all seasons, encroached upon its high places. Posts, and rails and old cautions to trespassers, and backs of mean houses, and patches of wretched vegetation, stared it out of countenance. Nothing was the better for it, or thought of being so. If the miserable waste ground lying near it could have laughed, it would have laughed it to scorn, like many of the miserable neighbours.

CHARLES DICKENS

13. THE CONDITION OF THE DEAD IN 1844

In Manchester, the pauper burial-ground lies opposite to the Old Town, along the Irk; this, too, is a rough, desolate place. About two years ago a railroad was carried through it. If it had been a respectable cemetery, how the bourgeoisie and the clergy would have shrieked over the desecration! But it was a pauper burial-ground, the resting-place of the outcast and the superfluous, so no one concerned himself about the matter. It was not even thought worth while to convey the partially decayed bodies to the other side of the cemetery; they were heaped up just as it happened, and piles were driven into newly-made graves, so that the water oozed out of the swampy ground, pregnant with putrefying matter, and filled the neighbourhood with the most revolting and injurious gases. The disgusting brutality which accompanied this work I cannot describe in further detail.

FRIEDRICH ENGELS

14. THE NAVIGATORS

THE labourers who executed these formidable works were in many respects a remarkable class. The "railway navvies," as they were called, were men drawn by the attraction of good wages from all parts of the kingdom; and they were ready for any sort of hard work. Many of the labourers employed on the Liverpool line were Irish, others were from the Northumberland and Durham railways, where they had been accustomed to similar work; and some of the best came from the fen districts of Lincoln and Cambridge where they had been trained to execute works of excavation and embankment. These old practitioners formed the nucleus of a skilled manipulation and aptitude, which rendered them of indispensable utility in the immense undertakings of the period. Their expertness in all sorts of earthwork, in embanking, boring, and well-sinking—their practical knowledge of the nature of soils and rocks, the tenacity of clays, and the porosity of certain stratifications—were very great; and, rough-looking as they were, many of them were as important in their own department as the contractor or the engineer.

During the railway-making period the navvy wandered about from one public work to another—apparently belonging to no country and having no home. He usually wore a white felt hat, the brim turned up all round—a headdress since become fashionable—a velveteen or jean square-tailed coat, a scarlet plush waistcoat with little black spots, and a bright-coloured handkerchief round his herculean neck, when, as often happened, it was not left entirely bare. His corduroy breeches were retained in position by a leathern strap round the waist, and tied and buttoned at the knee, displaying beneath a solid calf and foot firmly encased in strong high-laced boots. Joining together in a "butty gang," some ten or twelve of these men would take a contract to cut out and remove so much "dirt"—so they denominated earth-cutting —fixing their price according to the character of the "stuff," and the distance to which it had to be wheeled and tipped. The contract taken, every man put himself to his mettle: if any was found skulking, or not putting forth his full working power, he was ejected from the gang. Their powers of endurance were extraordinary. In times of emergency they would work for twelve and even sixteen hours, with only short intervals for meals; and the quantity of flesh-meat which they consumed was something enormous; but it was to their bones and muscles what coke is to the locomotive— the means of keeping up the steam.

When railway-making extended to France, the English contractors for the works took with them gangs of English navvies, with the usual plant, which included wheelbarrows. These the English navvy was accustomed to run out continuously, loaded with some three to four hundredweight of stuff, piled so high that he could barely see over the summit of the load the gang-board along which he wheeled his barrow; whereas the French navvy was contented with half the weight. Indeed, the French navvies on one occasion struck work because of the size of the barrows, and there was a dangerous *émeute*, which was only quelled by the aid of the military. The consequence was that the big barrows were abandoned to the English workmen, who earned nearly double the wages of the Frenchmen. The manner in which they stood to their work was matter of great surprise and wonderment to the French country people, who came crowding round them in their blouses, and, after gazing admiringly at their expert handling of the pick and mattock, and the immense loads of "dirt" which they wheeled out, would exclaim to each other, *"Mon Dieu, voila! voila ces Anglais, comme ils travaillent!"*

SAMUEL SMILES

15. SPIRITUALLY DESTITUTE

THE dread which such men as these spread throughout a rural community, was striking; nor was it without a cause. Depredations among the farms and fields of the vicinity were frequent. They injured everything they approached. From their huts to that part of the railway at which they worked, over corn or grass, tearing down embankments, injuring young plantations, making gaps in hedges, on they went, in one direct line, without regard to damage done or property invaded. Game disappeared from the most sacred preserves; game-keepers were defied; and country gentlemen who had imprisoned rustics by the dozen for violating the same law, shrunk in despair from the railway "navigator." They often committed the most outrageous acts in their drunken madness. Like dogs released from a week's confinement, they ran about and did not know what to do with themselves. They defied the law; broke open prisons; released their comrades, and slew policemen. The Scotch fought with the Irish, and the Irish attacked the Scotch; while the rural peace-officers, utterly inadequate to suppress the tumult, stood calmly by and waited the result. . . .

The "navigators," wanderers on the face of the earth, owning no tie and fearing no law; "were," said the Rev. St. George Sargent, "the most neglected and spiritually destitute people I ever met; ignorant of Bible religion and Gospel truth, infected with infidelity, and prone to revolutionary principles."

JOHN FRANCIS

16. SOCIALISTS?

"YOU tell us," a Parliamentary Committee once said to a clergyman, "that the railway navvies are mostly infidels.

Would you say that they are also socialists?" "In practice, yes; because though most of them appear to have wives, few of them are really married."

ANON

17. THE NAVVY AND THE LANDLADY

DURING the construction of the present London and North-Western Railway, a landlady at Hillmorton, near Rugby, of very sharp practice, which she had imbibed in dealings for many years with canal boatmen, was constantly remarking aloud that no navvy should ever "*do*" her; and although the railway was in her immediate neighbourhood, and although the navvies were her principal customers, she took pleasure on every opportunity in repeating the invidious remark.

It had, however, one fine morning scarcely left her large, full-blown, rosy lips, when a fine-looking young fellow, walking up to her, carrying in both hands a huge stone bottle, commonly called a "grey-neck," briefly asked her for "half a gallon of gin"; which was no sooner measured and poured in than the money was rudely demanded before it could be taken away.

On the navvy declining to pay the exorbitant price asked, the landlady, with a face like a peony, angrily told him he must either pay for the gin or *instantly* return it.

He silently chose the latter, and accordingly, while the eyes of his antagonist were wrathfully fixed upon his, he returned into her measure the half-gallon, and then quietly walked off; but having previously put into his grey-neck half a gallon of water, each party eventually found themselves in possession of half a gallon of gin and water; and, however either may have enjoyed the mixture, it is historically at Hillmorton that the landlady was never again heard unnecessarily to boast "that no navvy could 'do' her."

SIR FRANCIS HEAD

18. THE EGYPTIANS ECLIPSED

THUS has sprung into existence in a few years, a piece of human workmanship of the most stupendous kind; which, when considered with respect to its scientific character, magnitude, utility, its harmony of arrangement, and mechanical contrivance, eclipses all former works of art. Compared to it, how shabby a structure would be the celebrated Roman wall, or even the more extensive one of the Chinese; as for the Egyptian pyramids, they, so far from being fit to be mentioned in comparison with the railway, are merely uncouth monuments of the ignorance and superstition of their founders; woeful testimonials of the debasement to priestcraft of the wretched slaves who erected them, and are merely evidences of much physical force, having but little aid from science or taste.

GUIDE TO THE LONDON & BIRMINGHAM RAILWAY

19. THE QUEEN IS CHARMED

Buckingham Palace,
14th June, 1842

WE arrived here yesterday morning, having come by the railroad from Windsor, in half an hour, free from dust and crowd and heat, and I am quite charmed with it.

QUEEN VICTORIA

20. NOT QUITE SO FAST

PRINCE ALBERT invariably accompanies the Queen, but patronises the Great Western generally when compelled to come up from Windsor alone. The Prince, however, has been known to say, "Not quite so fast next time, Mr. Conductor, if you please."

MORNING POST, February 1842

21. SITUATION WANTED

DOUCEUR.—£20—The advertiser (a young man of respectability) will present the above sum to any lady or gentleman who will procure for the above a SITUATION as GUARD, Ticket Collector, etc., on any railway. The utmost secrecy may be relied on.

THE TIMES, 25 February 1852

22. BRANWELL BRONTE: TICKET-COLLECTOR

PAINTING and poetry alike had failed, but Branwell was anxious, or at least willing, to employ himself somehow, and in September he became the booking-clerk at a small station called Sowerby Bridge. It was a dismal *degringolade* from the brilliant promise of his boyhood and from the bright hopes which Charlotte, above all, had entertained about his career. . . . She writes (September 1840):

A distant relative of mine, one Patrick Boanerges, has set off to seek his fortune in the wild, wandering, adventurous, romantic, knight-errant-like capacity of clerk on the Leeds and Manchester Railroad.

E. F. BENSON

23. WHAT IMMORTAL HAND?

I CANNOT express the amazed awe, the crushed humility, with which I sometimes watch a locomotive take its breath at a railway station, and think what work there is in its bars and wheels, and what manner of men they must be who dig brown iron-stone out of the ground, and forge it into THAT! What assemblage of accurate and mighty faculties in them; more than fleshly power over melting crag and coiling fire, fettered, and finessed at last into the precision of watchmaking; Titan hammer-strokes beating, out of lava, these glittering cylinders and timely-respondent valves, and fine ribbed rods, which touch each other as a serpent writhes, in noiseless gliding, and omnipotence of grasp; infinitely complex anatomy of action steel, compared with which the skeleton of a living creature would seem, to a careless observer, clumsy and vile—a mere morbid secretion and phosphatous prop of flesh! What would the men who thought out this—who beat it out, who touched it into its polished calm of power, who set it to its appointed task, and triumphantly saw it fulfil this task to the utmost of their will—feel or think about this weak hand of mine, timidly leading a little stain of water-colour, which I cannot manage, into an imperfect shadow of something else—mere failure in every motion, and endless disappointment; what, I repeat, would these Iron-dominant Genii think of me? and what ought I to think of them?

JOHN RUSKIN

24. THE ENGINE

"On fire-horses and wind-horses we career."—CARLYLE

HURRAH! for the mighty engine,
    As he bounds along his track:
Hurrah, for the life that is in him,
    And his breath so thick and black.

And hurrah for our fellows, who in their need
    Could fashion a thing like him—
With a heart of fire, and a soul of steel,
    And a Samson in every limb.

Ho! stand from that narrow path of his,
    Lest his gleaming muscles smite,
Like the flaming sword the archangel drew
    When Eden lay wrapp'd in night;
For he cares, not he, for a paltry life
    As he rushes along to the goal,
It but costs him a shake of his iron limb,
    And a shriek from his mighty soul.

Yet I glory to think that I help to keep
    His footsteps a little in place,
And he thunders his thanks as he rushes on
    In the lightning speed of his race;
And I think that he knows when he looks at me,
    That, though made of clay as I stand,
I could make him as weak as a three hours' child
    With a paltry twitch of my hand.

But I trust in his strength, and he trusts in me,
    Though made but of brittle clay,
While he is bound up in the toughest of steel,
    That tires not night or day;
But for ever flashes, and stretches, and strives,
    While he shrieks in his smoky glee—
Hurrah for the puppets that, lost in their thoughts,
    Could rub the lamp for me.

Ay, give me the beat of his fire-fed breast,
    And the shake of his giant frame,

And the sinews that work like the shoulders of Jove
    When he launches a bolt of flame;
And give me that Lilliput rider of his,
    Stout and wiry and grim,
Who can vault on his back as he puffs his pipe,
    And whisk the breath from him.

Then hurrah for our mighty engine, boys;
    He may roar and fume along
For a hundred years ere a poet arise
    To shrine him in worthy song;
Yet if one with the touch of the gods on his lips,
    And his heart beating wildly and quick,
Should rush into song at this demon of ours,
    Let him sing, too, the shovel and pick.

ALEXANDER ANDERSON
Poet and Platelayer

25. R. I. P.

DIED, after a long and protracted existence, the near leader of the "Red Rover," the last of the London and Southampton coaches. The symptoms of decay, which ended in the event we now record, set in on the day the South Western Railway opened, the severe grief produced by which brought on an affection of the heart, which, acting upon a frame not of the strongest, induced the calamity so much deplored by the inconsolable proprietors.

ANON

26. THE RAILROAD

WHY! why to yon arch do the people drift,
Like a sea hurrying in to a cavern's rift,
Or like streams to a whirlpool streaming swift?
        'Tis the railroad!

Each street and each causeway endeth there;
And the whole of their peoples may step one stair
Down from the arch, and a power shall bear
Them swifter than wind from the mighty lair;
    'Tis the railroad!

Pass through the arch; put your ear to the ground!
This road sweepeth on through the isle and around!
You touch that which touches the country's bound!
    'Tis the railroad!
Like arrowy lightning snatch'd from the sky,
And bound to the earth, the bright rails lie;
And their way is straight driven through mountains
 high.
And headland to headland o'er valleys they tie;
    'Tis the railroad!

See how the engine hums still on the rails,
While his long train of cars slowly down to him sails;
He staggers like a brain blooded high, and he wails;
    'Tis the railroad!
His irons take the cars, and screaming he goes;
Now may heaven warn before him all friends and all
 foes!
A whole city's missives within him repose,
Half a thousand miles his, ere the day's hours close;
    'Tis the railroad!

       EBENEZER JONES

27. IN THE VAN OF TRUTH

Electric Line of thought connecting Man
Each unto each in wondrous brotherhood!
Chain of fraternal Love—as strong as blood

Which through all nations in one current ran
When first the mighty stream of life began,
—How canst thou then be anything but good?
I hail ye, Railways!—If not understood
As poetry, ye leave us in the van
Of truth!—Ay, even the laying bare the steps
And foot-prints of the Almighty as we cleave
Through strata deep—is an Apocalypse
Of wonder, that the spirit doth upheave
Sky-ward. At once ye link us with the Past,
And with some social Æra coming fast!

CHAUNCY HARE TOWNSHEND

28. LET THEM STAND!

WE do not feel disposed to attach much weight to the argument in favour of third-class carriages with seats. On a short
line little physical inconvenience can result from their absence.

THE RAILWAY TIMES

29. ARTIFICIAL INCONVENIENCES

"CERTAIN persons in superior positions" were base enough to
travel in third-class carriages. If universal indignation could
have crushed these miserable creatures, they would soon have
succumbed; but they persevered, even in spite of the "artificial inconveniences" specially invented to deter them. Not
but what these inconveniences were serious enough. The
management of the Manchester and Leeds Railway adopted
what was known as the "soot-bag system." Sweeps were
hired to enter a third-class carriage which had been specially
kept for the benefit of "persons in a superior position," and
then shake out the contents of their bags. At other times, if
a correspondent of the *Railway Times* can be trusted, "sheep

and sometimes pigs were made the substitutes for sweeps."
Even then some persons—if report said true some bailies of
the City of Glasgow—persevered in their evil courses. But
their conduct evidently was strongly reprehended by all
respectable persons. In describing the London and Black-
wall Railway, Mr. Whishaw, the engineer writes more in
sorrow than in anger, "We were astonished to see several
most respectably dressed persons riding in the Stanhope compartments, which are intended especially for those who cannot
afford to pay for better accommodation."

W. M. ACWORTH

30. PERSUASION

A PASSENGER by the second-class carriages on the Manchester
and Leeds complains that himself and a female relative have
caught a severe cold from the holes in the floors of the
carriages, which admit currents of air to the legs of passengers;
he asks if there is any use or object in these holes, except to
drive passengers into the first-class carriages. We cannot
answer him.

THE LEEDS MERCURY

31. THE TOURIST'S ALPHABET

A is the affable guard whom you square:
B is the *Bradshaw* which leads you to swear:
C is the corner you fight to obtain:
D is the draught of which others complain:
E are the enemies made for the day:
F is the frown that you wear all the way:
G is the guilt that you feel going third:
H is the humbug by which you're deterred:
I is the insult you'll get down the line:

J is the junction where you'll try to dine:
K is the kettle of tea three weeks old:
L are the lemon drops better unsold:
M is the maiden who says there's no meat:
N is the nothing you thus get to eat:
O is the oath that you use—and do right:
P is the paper to which you *don't* write:
Q are the qualms to directors unknown:
R is the row which you'll find all your own:
S is the smash that is "nobody's fault":
T is the truth, that will come to a halt:
U is the pointsman—who's up the whole night:
V is the verdict that says it's "all right."
W stands for wheels flying off curves:
X for express that half shatters your nerves:
Y for the yoke from your neck that you fling,
and Z for your zest as you cut the whole thing!

MR. PUNCH'S RAILWAY BOOK

32. THE WONDER OF THE AGE

(1)

A shrewd young working man named Stephenson,
Enlisting fire and water to his aid,
Devised a quicker way to get to London.
We are now fastened in a noisy box,
And seeing little of the lovely country,
And hearing little if we try to talk,
A puff of steam propels us like an arrow
Along an iron road, through dismal cuttings
And dreadful tunnels, to our journey's end.
A glorious victory of engineering,
By which we shorten time and travel cheaply,

So that where one used formerly to ride
A hundred now can go and see their friends.

(II)

The motto of our engineers is this:
"You give us money, we will give machinery
To execute whatever work you need."
And, truly, mighty marvels have been wrought;
For as it is our fools who own the money—
And there are many fools to one wise man—
The world must needs be greatly benefited.
Our railways are the wonder of the age;
It was our fools who chiefly paid for them,
And everybody rides at their expense.
We therefore have great cause to thank the fools;
We may have reason yet to thank them more,
And have a tunnel underneath the channel,
And railway trains, laden with sightseers,
Careering to and fro 'twixt France and England,
Making the different families of Europe
Better acquainted with each other's ways,
And thus promote the general harmony.
As the scared natives of some Indian shore
Gaze at the passing ship far out at sea,
And wonder what strange animal it is,
So did our country bumpkins open their mouths,
And stare to see the strange and wondrous sight,
When first a railway train went thundering through
The calm seclusion of a rural hamlet.

                                    JAMES HURNARD

33. HIS FIRST TOUR

I WAS an enthusiastic temperance man, and the secretary of a district association, which embraced parts of the two counties of Leicester and Northampton. A great meeting was to be held at Leicester, over which Lawrence Heyworth, Esq., of Liverpool—a great railway as well as temperance man—was advertised to preside. From my residence at Market Harborough I walked to Leicester (fifteen miles) to attend that meeting. About midway between Harborough and Leicester —my mind's eye has often reverted to the spot—a thought flashed through my brain, what a glorious thing it would be if the newly-developed powers of railways and locomotion could be made subservient to the promotion of temperance! That thought grew upon me as I travelled over the last six or eight miles. I carried it up to the platform, and, strong in the confidence of the sympathy of the chairman, I broached the idea of engaging a special train to carry the friends of temperance from Leicester to Loughborough and back to attend a quarterly delegate meeting appointed to be held there in the two or three weeks following. The chairman approved, the meeting roared with excitement, and early next day I proposed my grand scheme to John Fox Bell, the resident secretary of the Midland Counties Railway Company. Mr. Paget, of Loughborough, opened his park for a gala, and on the day appointed about five hundred passengers filled some twenty or twenty-five open carriages—they were called "tubs" in those days—and the party rode the enormous distance of eleven miles and back for a shilling, children half-price. We carried music with us, and music met us at the Loughborough station. The people crowded the streets, filled windows, covered the house-tops, and cheered us all along the line, with the heartiest welcome. All went off in the best style and in perfect safety we returned to Leicester; and thus was struck the keynote of my excursions, and the social idea grew upon me.

THOMAS COOK

34. THE MANIA

LONDON, November 16th [1845]—It has been during the last two months that the rage for railroad speculation reached its height, was checked by a sudden panic in full career, and is now reviving again, though not by any means promising to recover its pristine vigour. I met one day in the middle of it the Governor of the Bank at Robarts', who told me that he never remembered in all his experience anything like the present speculation; that the operations of '25, which led to the great panic, were nothing to it, and that there could not fail to be a fearful reaction. . . . It is incredible how people have been tempted to speculate; half the fine ladies have been dabbling in stocks, and men the most unlikely have not been able to refrain from gambling in shares, even I myself (though in a very small degree), for the warning voice of the Governor of the Bank has never been out of my ears.

CHARLES GREVILLE

35. THE MANIA SPREADS

THE most cautious were deceived by this apparent prosperity; and men esteemed good citizens and sound moralists were drawn into acts which avarice urged but conscience condemned. They saw their neighbour's establishment increasing; they heard the cry of railways at every turn; they listened to speeches at dinners, uttered by solemn, solid men, upon the glories of the rail; they read of princes mounting tenders, of peers as provisional committee men, of marquises trundling wheelbarrows, and of privy councillors cutting turf "on correct geometrical principles." Their clerks left them to become railway jobbers. Their domestic servants studied railway journals. Men were pointed out in the streets who had made their tens of thousands. They saw the whole world railway mad. The iron road was extolled at public meetings; it was the object of public worship; it was talked of on the exchange; legislated for in the senate; satirised on the stage. It penetrated every class; it permeated every household; and all yielded to the temptation. Men who went to church as devoutly as to their counting-houses—men whose word had ever been as good as their bond—joined the pursuit. They entered the whirlpool, and were carried away by the vortex. They first cautiously wrote for shares in the names of their children, and sold the letters at a price which, while it consoled them for present turpitude, tempted them to fresh sin.

JOHN FRANCIS

36. THE IRON WEB

THROUGHOUT the decade of the eighteen-forties he [Mr. Milnes, senior] was deeply and successfully engaged in trying to recoup his family's fortunes by means of the railway boom. 1845 was the peak year of the railway speculation which had seized upon the whole nation in much the same way as the eighteenth-century South Sea Bubble. In November 1845 *The Times* newspaper, which was striving to expose the railway scandals, published an analysis showing that over 1,200 railway lines had been projected by private companies and that the total capital investment required from members of the public amounted to £500,000,000. A great number of these lines were competing with each other; many of them were unnecessary; several of them were impracticable; a few

were outright swindles. Greville noted in his diary for this
year how wild the speculation had become, how unsafe yet
how wholly irresistible. The attention of members of Parliament was soon distracted by service on one or other of the
numberless railway investigation committees set up (in the
temporary wooden sheds used as committee rooms at Westminster) to try and protect the public and save the country
from transport chaos, and from what Richard Monckton
Milnes called "the confused net of iron" which was being
spread all across the English counties. Milnes himself served
on one of these committees:

> The extent of railroad speculation has been perfectly
> awful [he wrote in June 1845], and the loss will be pro-
> portionate. The lobbies of the House of Commons have
> been like an Exchange, with carrier pigeons going off to
> the City with the decisions and turns of Committees.
> Mine has now sat six weeks.

Three months before this he had published an article pointing
out the aesthetic merits of the French and Italian railroad
projects, which were being built with English labour and
English capital, but were designed by foreigners and with a
view to the landscape:

> the one from Rouen to Paris [he wrote] keeps crossing
> the Seine like a huge snake lying over its course, and
> exhibits a series of continuous pleasant rural pictures
> such as we hardly know of on any English line.

He suggested, too, that when the whole continent was made
"permeable" to English travellers, the political effects might
be considerable.

> When . . . we are all well jolted together in the same
> train, the *entente cordiale* will perhaps be closer than it is

now. No longer will the English carriage roll through the plains of Touraine and Auvergne in all its solitary pomposity, with the lady's maid indignant at not stopping regularly for tea at four o'clock in a housekeeper's room, and the courier as pretentious as an Eastern dragoman: no longer will the steamer descend the Rhone with the light freight of one English family, taking the boat to themselves to avoid the annoyance of continental contact.

But English people in 1845 did not like being told home truths any more than they do today. Milnes' views were dismissed as just one more example of his love of paradox. Railway construction, unplanned, unchecked, went fast ahead.

The Milnes' estates at Bawtry and Fryston, at Fishlake and Thorne, lay right across the routes of at least seven of the projected railways. With the companies directing six of these Mr. Milnes concluded very satisfactory negotiations. The seventh company, that of the Great or Direct Northern, which had absorbed the original London-and-York project, proved tougher to deal with; but even so Mr. Milnes netted a round sum of £100,000 in a few years. The most spectacular personality in the railway boom was George Hudson, the "Railway King." Hudson was a Yorkshire farmer's son whose extraordinary enterprise had swept him from the position of apprentice to a York draper to that of a millionaire railway magnate, a Member of Parliament, and builder of two vast and lavish houses in Albert Gate, Hyde Park. Richard Milnes and his father both liked Hudson; and for many years after the crash which ended his career they remembered him and tried to help his impoverished wife and family. Though ready to laugh at the accents and education of the railway magnates and their wives, the Milneses, like most other landowning families in England, were only too ready to profit by these new phenomena. Indeed, the land-owning class showed itself, in these years, quite as astute at money-making as any of the hard-headed new rich. Mr. Milnes always suspected the railway companies of trying to get the better of him. He liked to prolong and complicate negotiations until he had screwed out the last penny for his land. He would confront the company promoters with a mixture of efficient financial sense and well-bred charm which was most disarming. After a deal with George Hudson involving tens of thousands of pounds, he added a postscript to a letter to Richard: " I said to H.," he wrote, "that whatever it is, it must be *guineas*, as I mean to give the shillings to my wife. He said, 'by all means'."

Although they had an unusual chance to make big sums of money, the landowners' position during these negotiations remained a little delicate. On the one hand, as much land as possible should be sold to the railways as expensively as possible, before the bubble burst and values dropped (a process which began in 1847). On the other hand, the line must not pass too close to one's own house or ruin the appearance of one's estate. Together with his daughter's husband, Galway, Mr. Milnes became a positive authority on engineering in these years. He would decide where stations should go, whether a line ought to take a high or a low bank, how a plantation or a willow-bed could be saved, a lodge moved, or a tunnel dug under the village of Brotherton. At one moment the best course for a new line seemed to him to be slap through the middle of Byram, his neighbours' house across the Aire, at another a deviation behind Ferry Fryston church seemed most desirable. Although his advice was not always taken by the railway companies, it amused him to give it; and in these days Fryston rang with talk of viaducts and deviations, loops and halts, the merits of the Sheffield-and-Manchester as against the Leeds-and-Bradford. He would make sketch-maps on little scraps of paper or count up the number of passengers on some new express train to show that in the end the passenger traffic could never pay. Born into the easy coaching world of the late eighteenth century, he showed a remarkable adaptability in assimilating the conditions of the new steam age. Mrs. Milnes was less enthusiastic about the railroads. She wrote to ask Richard never to cross the line at a level-crossing, citing the recent Brighton accident in which a "young person" had been knocked down by an engine (the severed head being afterwards found inside her bonnet beside the track). A female cottager at Castleford had cried out against the railways as Mr. Milnes was passing by: "Oh, the railroad, the horrid railroad, do promise me, Mr. Milnes, that you will stop it." In Ferrybridge the five coaching inns were already on the decline as wheeled traffic on the Great North Road fell off. Of fifty pair of post-horses only three were left by the end of the decade, and one of the three postboys (so Mr. Milnes said) had hanged himself. All over England the iron web was spinning. For the first time movement from one end of the country to the other was becoming quick and easy for the rich and possible for the poor.

JAMES POPE-HENNESSY

37. THE GREAT LEVELLER

MANY, if not most, of the distinctive phenomena that constitute "the nineteenth century" are directly due to railway speed, that is, we can scarcely imagine the possibility of their development in the absence of railways. As shrewd Mr. Edward Pease said seventy years ago, "Let the country but make the railroads, and the railroads will make the country"; and they *have* made the country, for better or worse, moulded the leading features of its national life. Let us glance at a few haphazard instances.

First, for people who are nothing if not Socialistic, consider the unexampled *diffusion of wealth* in the last forty years; an unexampled *diffusion*, however striking may be the contrast still between the very rich and very poor. This is shown by the wonderful approach towards uniformity of *prices* in different parts; goods instantly move from where they are most plentiful, and this quicksilver action could never have occurred before railways. Railways have made everything *common*.

And the people of different localities are getting to vary almost as little as the prices; there is a uniformity of "common" manners, it is said. The immediate effect does seem to be this. Still, railways have introduced *freedom*, and from this will, later on, develop unimagined *individuality*. When "a penny a mile" came in all feudal links with the past were snapped, including the traditional deference to surroundings from which one saw no means of escape; the abrupt freedom has produced an "independence" of manners which is no doubt "commoner," but perhaps not more unsatisfactory, than the laboured insincerity of former times. The railway has made the poor "stand up to" the rich much as Luther stirred the nations to defy the Church.

This modern freedom must be held responsible for a great deal of our "realistic" tendency in art and behaviour; people demand the genuine and true rather than the picturesque or sentimental.

E. FOXWELL AND T. C. FARRER

Up Trains, Down Trains

38. RED LIGHT

I SEE no reason to suppose that these machines will ever force themselves into general use.

DUKE OF WELLINGTON

NOTHING is more distasteful to me than to hear the echo of our hills reverberating with the noise of hissing railroad engines, running through the heart of our hunting country, and destroying the noble sport which I have been accustomed to from my childhood.

MR. BERKELEY, M.P.

NEXT to a civil war, railways are the greatest curse to the country.

COL. SIBTHORPE, M.P.

HE expressed his pain that they had made arrangements for conveying foreigners and others to Cambridge at such fares as might be likely to tempt persons who having no regard for Sunday themselves would inflict their presence on the University on that day of rest. . . . The contemplated arrangements were as distasteful to the University authorities as they must be offensive to Almighty God and to all right minded Christians.

DR. G. E. CORRIE, Master of Jesus College
(Reported in the *Cambridge Chronicle*, 1851)

IN all countries where railroads exist they are considered a very dangerous mode of locomotion, and, beyond those who have very urgent business to transact, no one thinks of using them.

A CHINESE GENTLEMAN

I WOULD no more trust the railway proprietors on railway matters, than I would Gracchus speaking of sedition.

WILLIAM EWART GLADSTONE

*

39. GREEN LIGHT

THE increasing powers of Steam which like you I look on "half proud half sad half angry and half pleased" in doing so much for the commercial world promise something also for the sociable, and like Prince Housseins tapestry will I think one day waft friends together in the course of a few hours and for aught we may be able to [tell] bring Hampstead and Abbotsford within the distance of "will you dine with us quietly tomorrow."

SIR WALTER SCOTT

I REJOICE to see it, and to think that feudality is gone for ever: it is so great a blessing to think that any one evil is really extinct.

DR. ARNOLD

VIRTUE is the child of Knowledge: Vice of Ignorance: therefore education, periodical literature, railroad travelling, ventilation, drainage and the arts of life, when fully carried out,
serve to make a population moral and happy.

CARDINAL NEWMAN

*

40. LOCKED UP WITH WIDOWS

"I CON-SIDER," said Mr. Weller, "that the rail is uncon-
stitootional and an inwaser o' priwileges, and I should wery
much like to know what that 'ere old Carter as once stood up
for our liberties and wun 'em too,—I should like to know wot
he vould say, if he wos alive now, to Englishmen being
locked up vith widders, or vith anybody again their wills.
Wot a old Carter vould have said, a old Coachman may say,
and I as-sert that in that pint o' view alone, the rail is an
inwaser. As to the comfort, vere's the comfort o' sittin' in a
harm-cheer lookin' at brick walls or heaps o' mud, never
comin' to a public-house, never seein' a glass o' ale, never
goin' through a pike, never meetin' a change o' no kind
(horses or othervise), but alvays comin' to a place, ven you
come to one at all, the wery picter o' the last, vith the same
p'leesemen standin' about, the same blessed old bell a ringin',
the same unfort'nate people standin' behind the bars, a
waitin' to be let in; and everythin' the same except the name,
vich is wrote up in the same sized letters as the last name, and
vith the same colours. As to the *h*onour and dignity o'
travellin', vere can that be vithout a coachman; and wot's
the rail to sich coachmen and guards as is sometimes forced
to go by it, but a outrage and a insult? As to the pace, wot
sort o' pace do you think I, Tony Veller, could have kept a
coach goin' at for five hundred thousand pound a mile, paid
in adwance afore the coach was on the road? And as to the
ingein,—a nasty, wheezin', creakin', gaspin', puffin', bustin'

monster, alvays out o' breath vith a shiny green-and-gold back, like a unpleasant beetle in that 'ere gas magnifier,—as to the ingein as is alvays a pourin' out red-hot coals at night, and black smoke in the day, the sensiblest thing it does, in my opinion, is, ven there's somethin' in the vay, and it sets up that 'ere frightful scream vich seems to say, 'Now here's two hundred and forty passengers in the wery greatest extremity o' danger, and here's their two hundred and forty screams in vun!'"

CHARLES DICKENS

41. STEAM RAISES THE DEVIL

AND as if the old mail coach rate of eight miles an hour was not fast enough for the march of civilisation, the devil has been raised in the shape of steam to impel us at his own pace. You remember the proverb "Needs must go when *he* drives." One of the worst things attending this revolution in public travelling is, it leaves you no choice. At this time there is only one coach, which runs from Manchester to London. The Birmingham Railway has already produced this effect, and an utter recklessness to the convenience and safety of the passengers is one consequence of the monopoly which has thus been gained. The confusion when the luggage of a whole train is thrown down at the end of its course is said to exceed anything one has ever seen of this kind. As to personal safety, there must be less danger than in an overloaded coach, and there is also less fatigue in the motion itself, to say nothing of the great saving in that respect by going twenty miles an hour, instead of eight. But, after all, slow and sure would be more to my liking. My pleasantest, or I might better say happiest, travels have been either at a mule's foot-pace, or with a knapsack on my own shoulders.

ROBERT SOUTHEY

42. YOU FOOLS EVERYWHERE

THERE was a rocky valley between Buxton and Bakewell, once upon a time, divine as the Vale of Tempe: you might have seen the gods there morning and evening—Apollo and all the sweet Muses of the light—walking in fair procession on the lawns of it, and to and fro among the pinnacles of its crags. You cared neither for Gods nor grass, but for cash (which you did not know the way to get); you thought you would get it by what *The Times* calls "Railroad Enterprise." You Enterprised a Railroad through the valley, you blasted its rocks away, heaped thousands of tons of shale into its lovely stream. The valley is gone, and the Gods with it; and now, every fool in Buxton can be at Bakewell in half an hour, and every fool in Bakewell at Buxton; which you think a lucrative process of exchange—you Fools everywhere.

JOHN RUSKIN

YOUR middle-class man thinks it the highest pitch of development and civilisation when his letters are carried twelve times a day from Islington to Camberwell, and from Camberwell to Islington, and if railway-trains run to and fro between them every quarter of an hour. He thinks it nothing that the trains only carry him from an illiberal, dismal life at Islington to an illiberal, dismal life at Camberwell; and the letters only tell him that such is the life there.

MATTHEW ARNOLD

43. ON THE PROJECTED KENDAL AND WINDERMERE RAILWAY

Is then no nook of English ground secure
From rash assault? Schemes of retirement sown
In youth, and 'mid the busy world kept pure
As when their earliest flowers of hope were blown,

Must perish;—how can they this blight endure?
And must he too the ruthless change bemoan
Who scorns a false utilitarian lure
'Mid his paternal fields at random thrown?
Baffle the threat, bright Scene, from Orrest-head
Given to the pausing traveller's rapturous glance:
Plead for thy peace, thou beautiful romance
Of nature; and, if human hearts be dead,
Speak, passing winds; ye torrents, with your strong
And constant voice, protest against the wrong.

WILLIAM WORDSWORTH

44. CONSTERNATION AT RYDAL

Rydal Mount, Oct. 15th, 1844

MY DEAR MR. GLADSTONE,

We are in this neighbourhood all in consternation, that is every man of taste and feeling, at the stir which is made for carrying a branch Railway from Kendal to the head of Windermere. When the subject comes before you officially, as I suppose it will, pray give it more attention than its apparent importance may call for. In fact, the project if carried into effect will destroy the *staple* of the Country which is its beauty, and, on the Lord's day particularly, will prove subversive of its quiet, and be highly injurious to its morals. At present I shall say no more, only let me beg of you to cast your eye over a letter which I propose shortly to address thro' the public Press to our two county Members upon the occasion.

Believe me my dear Mr. Gladstone
faithfully your much obliged

WM. WORDSWORTH

45. SINCERE FLATTERY OF W.W.

POETIC LAMENTATION ON THE INSUFFICIENCY OF STEAM LOCOMOTION IN THE LAKE DISTRICT

Bright Summer spreads his various hue
    O'er nestling vales and mountains steep,
Glad birds are singing in the blue,
    In joyous chorus bleat the sheep.
But men are walking to and fro,
    Are riding, driving far and near,
And nobody as yet can go
    By train to Buttermere.

The sunny lake, the mountain track,
    The leafy groves are little gain,
While Rydal's pleasant pathways lack
    The rattle of the passing train.
But oh! what poet would not sing
    That heaven-kissing rocky cone,
On whose steep side the railway king
    Should set his smoky throne?

Helvellyn in those happy days
    With tunnelled base and grimy peak
Will mark the lamp's approaching rays,
    And hear the whistle's warning shriek:
Will note the coming of the mails,
    And watch with unremitting stare
The dusky grove of iron rails
    Which leads to Euston-square.

Wake, England, wake! 'tis now the hour
    To sweep away this black disgrace—
The want of locomotive power
    In so enjoyable a place.

Nature has done her part, and why
    Is mightier man in his to fail?
I want to hear the porters cry,
    "Change here for Ennerdale!"

Man! nature must be sought and found
    In lonely pools, on verdant banks;
Go, fight her on her chosen ground,
    Turn shapely Thirlmere into tanks:
Pursue her to her last retreats,
    And if perchance a garden plot
Is found among the London streets,
    Smoke, steam and spare it not.

Presumptuous nature! do not rate
    Unduly high thy humble lot,
Nor vainly strive to emulate
    The fame of Stephenson and Watt.
The beauties which thy lavish pride
    Has scattered through the smiling land
Are little worth till sanctified
    By man's completing hand.

J. K. STEPHEN

46. TRING IS SO BRACING

An impression is current that this method of travelling is injurious to health. We cannot suppose that our readers are influenced by such prejudices; and we believe that it is a work of supererogation, to apply other than the language of ridicule to such an absurd notion; but should any timid person hesitate in such matter, we quote the opinion of Dr. James Johnson, a physician of first rate talent and deserved eminence, to cure any apprehensions which he may entertain. Contrasting Railway travelling with that by Coach, the Doctor says, "The former equalises the circulation, promotes digestion, tranquillises the nerves, and often causes sound sleep during the succeeding night; the exercise of this kind of travelling being unaccompanied by that lassitude, aching and fatigue, which, in weakly constitutions, is the invariable accompaniment of ordinary travelling; and which so frequently, in such constitutions, produces sleepless nights."

"The Railroads bid fair to be a powerful remedial agent in many ailments to which the metropolitan and civic inhabitants are subject; and to thousands of valetudinarians in the Metropolis, the ride to Tring and back twice or three times a week, *would prove a means of preserving health, and prolonging life, more than all the Drugs in Apothecaries' Hall.*"

ANON

47. VERILY RAILWAYS ARE ABOMINATIONS

AFTER we had looked at the Church for a little time we mounted the omnibus to go to the railway station where we were to take train to Rouen—it was about 5 miles I should think from Louviers to the station. What a glorious ride that was, with the sun, which was getting low by that time, striking all across the valley that Louviers lies in; I think that valley was the most glorious of all we saw that day, there was not much grain there, it was nearly all grass land and the trees, O! the trees! it was all like the country in a beautiful poem, in a beautiful Romance such as might make a background to Chaucer's Palamon and Arcite; how we could see the valley winding away along the side of the Eure a long way, under the hills: but we had to leave it and go to Rouen by a nasty, brimstone, noisy, shrieking railway train that cares not twopence for hill or valley, poplar tree or lime tree, corn poppy, or blue cornflower, or purple thistle and purple vetch, white convolvulus, white clematis, or golden S. John's wort; that cares not twopence either for tower, or spire, or apse, or dome, till it will be as noisy and obtrusive under the spires of Chartres or the towers of Rouen, as it is under Versailles or the Dome of the Invalides, verily railways are ABOMINATIONS; and I think I have never fairly realised this fact till this our tour: fancy, Crom, all the roads (or nearly all) that come into Rouen dip down into the valley where it lies, from gorgeous hills which command the most splendid views of Rouen, but we, coming into Rouen by railway, crept into it in the most seedy way, seeing actually nothing at all of it till we were driving through the town in an omnibus.

WILLIAM MORRIS

NEWCASTLE AND CARLISLE RAILWAY.
No._____   o'Clock,   _____ 1836.

From Carlisle to Hexham.

1st Class—Paid 6s. 6d.

This Ticket will be required on your Arrival at your Destination.
NOTICE.—No Fees allowed to be taken by any Guard, Porter, or other Servant of the Company.

Rails Around the World

48. AN ITALIAN TRIBUTE

A LA GLORIA IMPERITURA DI GIORGIO STEPHENSON
I FERROVIARII DI POGGI BONZI

Inscription at the station of Poggi Bonzi, near Florence

49. THE LAND OF THE PROUD MAMELUKE

BUT we must not confine our views to London, or Liverpool, or Manchester; there can be no question that foreign countries will adopt the Rail-way communication, as one great step in mechanical improvement and commercial enterprise. France and Germany, and America, have already their Rail-ways, and the Pasha of Egypt may be expected to follow close on the heels of his brother potentates. The country of the Pyramids, of Memphis, and of Thebes, shall then be celebrated for Rail-ways and Steam Carriages; the land of the proud Mameluke, or the wandering Arab, of Sphynxes and

Mummies, will become the theatre of mechanical invention, science, and the arts. The stately Turk, with his turban and slippers, will quit his couch and his carpet to mount his engine of fire and speed, that he may enjoy the delight of modern locomotion. So long is it since the reward was offered to the in~entor of a new pleasure, that some scepticism were excusable as to the possibility of any great and novel excitement. But the Locomotive Engine and Rail-way were reserved for the present day. From West to East, and from North to South, the mechanical principle, the philosophy of the nineteenth century, will spread and extend itself. The world has received a new impulse.

HENRY BOOTH

50. PECULIARITIES OF CONTINENTAL RAILWAYS

CONTINENTAL railways have peculiarities unknown in this country, which appear very strange, and are sometimes rather annoying, to Mr. Bull when he crosses the channel. In England, the traveller goes to the station when he pleases, lounges in the waiting-room, consumes Banbury-cakes, and drinks scalding coffee *ad libitum*, wanders about the platform, and superintends his own luggage, and, in fact, so long as he does not interfere with the convenience of other people, and does not violate the "bye-laws" of the Company, he may do what he likes without let or hindrance. In France the system is very different: instead of the traveller managing himself, he is managed. On procuring his ticket, he delivers up his luggage, pays a *sou* or two, and obtains a receipt, and is then marched into a waiting-room, according to the class of his fare; as if the Company were afraid that, having paid his money, he should not have his ride. When the train is ready, the first-class passengers are liberated, and every one scrambles to his seat with as much agility as circumstances will admit; the second-class travellers follow; and the third are then allowed to deposit themselves in the vehicles provided for their reception. The second-class carriages have the advantage of being lined with ticking, and are quite as comfortable as the old stage-coaches used to be in this country; but the speed of the trains is only about twenty miles an hour. Some of the officials have a grotesque appearance. Instead of the neatness and simple efficiency by which those functionaries are characterized in our own land, they wear a blue cotton blouse like the country people, to which is added a red belt, and a long, slouching, broad-brimmed hat like the priests. As men of authority, they of course wear swords, and they wield red signal-flags and horns, which give them the combined characteristics of the countryman, the soldier, the priest, and the huntsman. Whether any or all of these peculiarities in the arrangements of our Gallic neighbours are deserving of imitation on the railways of Old England, we leave to the decision of our readers. It is worthy of remark, that the stations and the provision made for the accommodation of passengers are in general superior to those in this country.

FREDERICK S. WILLIAMS

51. THE CZAR'S ROUTE

WHEN the Emperor Nicholas of Russia was asked to decide upon the route of the line between St. Petersburg and Moscow he contemptuously tossed aside the plans placed before him, ordered a map to be unrolled on the table, put his sword across the map, and drawing a straight line from one city to the other, regardless alike of rights of way and rights of property, flung his inexorable plan to the astounded surveyor, saying, "Voilà votre chemin de fer."

JOHN PENDLETON

52. TO THE GRAND DUKE CZAREVICH . . .

YOUR IMPERIAL HIGHNESS!

Having given the order to build a continuous line of railway across Siberia, which is to unite the rich Siberian provinces with the railway system of the Interior, I entrust to you to declare My will, upon your entering the Russian dominions after your inspection of the foreign countries of the East. At the same time, I desire you to lay the first stone at Vladivostok for the construction of the Siberian Railway, which is to be carried out at the cost of the State and under direction of the Government.

I remain your sincerely loving

ALEXANDER

53. VOILÀ VOTRE CHEMIN DE FER

OMSK. II class station. Buffet. Is situated within 3 versts of the town.

The climate is unfavourable, being characterised by a very dry air, an unsteady temperature with extreme changes from cold to heat and continuous winds, which in winter produce blizzards and in summer raise clouds of dust. The maximum temperature in Omsk is $+36\cdot4°$, the minimum $-41\cdot1°$.

The monotonous architecture of the small wooden buildings, the unpaved streets with wooden sidewalks, the absence of any vegetation, which perishes on the saline soil, give to Omsk the aspect of a large Cossack settlement . . . The town includes two gardens, one on the banks of the Om, organised by the Society for the Promotion of Elementary Education. A birch wood, situated on the northern side of the town within a verst of it, is the object of walks by the inhabitants. On the southern side near the railway line is another birch wood with a sanitary station, where Kirgiz yurtas are pitched for those who wish to drink kumys prepared under the supervision of the railway physicians.

At the edge of the fortress near the ramparts on the Om, stood a wooden penal prison surrounded by high stockades which, from the middle of the XVII century, was a centre for convicts banished from Russia. In 1849, the great Russian writer and thinker F. M. Dostoevsky (1821–1881) was condemned to hard labour for a period of four years, and was banished to this prison, for having played a part in the political affair of Petrashevsky. Recollections of this imprisonment with a description of the convict prison were recorded with great talent by Dostoevsky in his "Memoirs from a Dead House." This historical house has not existed for a long time, and the spot on which it formerly stood is occupied by new buildings.

Hotels and furnished rooms: Shchepanov's rooms for travellers from R.1 to R.2 a day. Zaitsev's rooms are the best; they are newly opened, provided with water and good dinners and cost from 75 K to R.3 a day. Next follow Veselovsky's, Vodzinsky's, Sametnikov's.

Hackney coach tariff: First class (open and closed carriages with two horses) 75 K an hour. Second class (a kind of victoria and little carts with springs), in winter 20 K an hour, in summer 25 K.

The station of Omsk holds an important place in the West-Siberian railway line on account of its dimensions; besides the passengers' station, there are over 70 buildings for the requirements of the railway. A large stone church in honour of the Holy Trinity, to hold 750 people, is being erected near the station. Besides the main track, the station has several sidings to meet the necessities of its extensive operations: a passenger way 300·31 sazhens long, a goods way 959·47 sazhens long. In 1898, the export of grain conveyed from this station to the interior markets of the Empire was given at 496,373 puds.

GUIDE TO THE GREAT SIBERIAN RAILWAY

54. RAILWAYS AND POWER POLITICS

CHINESE produce and merchandise were carried from one part to another of the country long before the Occidental world became civilised. But as China, owing to her geographical position and her endowment of abundant resources for self-support was absolutely cut off from the rest of the world for so long a time past, no impetus was given to her to develop fully her systems of communication. On the contrary, internal communication has been gradually falling into greater and greater neglect. The defective condition of communication kills trade on its way inland and paralyses the authority of Peking a few hundred miles from the capital.

Foreign nations have, one after another, closed in upon China both by land and by sea. . . . Above all, they have demanded concessions of rights for construction and even control of railways in order to increase their own resources through the absorption or exploitation of the undeveloped but vast and wealthy realm of the Celestial Empire. Several foreign nations, principally Russia, Germany, France, Great Britain and later, Japan, have taken an aggressive part in this movement. Concession after concession was forced out of the hands of the Peking Government. Railway concessions, standing above all others in value, have been and are still most eagerly sought and retained because railways can be used politically to strengthen the concessionaires' hold on China as well as to develop commercially their concessions of mines and other enterprises. In modern times the railway is the best and most effective instrument for colonization and for accomplishing the policy of imperial expansion. It is no wonder, therefore, that international politics in China are mostly railway politics.

MONGTON CHIH HSU

55. DRILL, YE TARRIERS, DRILL!

Ev'ry morning at seven o'clock
There were twenty tarriers working at the rock,
And the boss comes along, and he says, kape still,
And come down heavy on the cast-iron drill,
And drill, ye tarriers, drill!

The boss was a fine man down to the ground,
And he married a lady six feet round.
She baked good bread and she baked it well,
But she baked it hard as the holes in hell,
And drill, ye tarriers, drill!

The new foreman was Jean McCann,
By God, he was a blame mean man.
Last week a premature blast went off,
And a mile in the air went big Jim Goff,
And drill, ye tarriers, drill!

When the next pay day came round,
Jim Goff a dollar short was found.
When he asked, "What for?" came this reply,
"You're docked for the time you was up in the sky."
And drill, ye tarriers, drill!

Chorus: Drill, ye tarriers, drill!
It's work all day
For sugar in your tay;
Down behind of the railway,
And drill, ye tarriers, drill,
And blast! and fire!

AMERICAN FOLK-SONG

56. DRIVING THE LAST SPIKE

ALL the bells in all the great cities of the United States rang out jubilant peals as the last stroke sent home the last spike on the last rail of the new highway of travel. The news was flashed by telegraph everywhere throughout the Union, and that there might be no delay in its transmission and no hindrance to its simultaneous reception, a certain pre-arranged signal was given and all the wires were for the time being kept free of other business. There were cases in which, to save time in ringing out the glad news, the message was conveyed on special wires right up to the bell towers; and everywhere there was a feeling that a great victory had been won. Preceding the consummation, there had been some wonderful feats in railroad construction. From the Missouri river on the one side and from the Sacramento on the other, the two companies—the Union Pacific and the Central Pacific—advanced against each other in friendly rivalry. The popular idea was that the length of the line of each company would be measured to the point at which it joined rails with the other. . . . The greater part of the Union Pacific route was over comparatively even ground, and it was not until the Salt Lake region was being approached that any serious constructive difficulties presented themselves. It was otherwise with the company advancing eastward. The line had to be carried over the Sierra Nevada, the ascent beginning almost from the starting point, and rising seven thousand feet in a hundred miles. On the other side of the mountain range, the descent was in turn formidable. Over this part of the road it was impossible to proceed rapidly. The work was surrounded with difficulties, and there were competent engineers who had no confidence that it could be carried out. Progress could only be made at the outset at the rate of about twenty miles each year; but in this slow work there was time to profit by experience, so that eventually, when it became a question simply of many hands, the platelayer went forward with the swing of an army on the march. Then it was that the two companies went vigorously into the race of construction. In one day, in 1868, the Union men were able to inform the Central men by telegraph that they had laid as many as six miles since morning. A few days afterwards the response came from the Central men that they had just finished as their day's work a stretch of seven miles. Spurred to fresh activity by this display, the Union men next reported to the other side a complete stretch for a day's work of seven and a half miles! The answer came back in the extraordinary announcement that the workers for the Central Company were prepared to lay ten miles in one day! The Union people were inclined to regard this as mere boasting, and the Vice-President of the company implied as much when he made an offer to bet ten thousand dollars that in one day such a stretch of railroad could not be well and truly laid. It is not on record that the bet was taken up. But the fact remains that it was made, that the Central army of workers heard of it, and that they determined to make good the pledge given in their name. So a day was fixed for the attempt. From the Union side men came to take note of the work and to measure it, and their verdict at the close of the day's toil was that not only had the promised ten miles been constructed, but that the measurement showed two hundred feet over! . . .

In this great feat of construction more than four thousand men found employment in various capacities. When they had carried their line four miles further east, the Central and the Union men met each other, the point of connection being known as Promontory. The event took place on Monday, March 10th, 1869. Representatives were present from almost every part of the Union, and the construction parties, not yet wholly dispersed, made up a greater crowd than had been seen at Promontory before or is likely ever to be seen there again—for, with the fixing of the termini at another point, the glory of the place has departed. The connecting tie had been made of Californian laurel. It was beautifully polished, and bore a series of inscribed silver plates. The tie was carefully placed, and over it the rails were laid by picked men on behalf of each company. The spikes were then inserted—one of gold, silver, and iron, from Arizona; another of silver from Nevada; and a third of gold, from California. President Stanford, of the Central Pacific, armed with a hammer of solid silver, drove the last spike, the blow falling precisely at noon, and the news of the completion of the road being flashed abroad as it fell. Then the two locomotives, one from the west and the other from the east, drew up to each other on the single line, coming into gentle collision, that they in their way, in the pleasing conceit of their drivers, might symbolise the fraternisation that went on. It does not spoil the story of the ceremony to state that the laurel tie, with its inscriptions and its magnificent mountings, was only formally laid, and that it became from that day a relic to be officially cherished; and it should be added that the more serviceable tie which replaced it was cut into fragments by men eager to have some memento of the occasion. Other ties for a time shared the same fate, until splinters of what was claimed to be "the last tie laid" became as common as pieces of the Wellington boots the great commander is said to have left behind him at Waterloo. . . .

LEEDS MERCURY, 28 April 1881

57. DICKENS IN AMERICA

I MADE acquaintance with an American railroad on this occasion, for the first time. As these works are pretty much alike all through the States, their general characteristics are easily described.

There are no first- and second-class carriages as with us; but there is a gentlemen's car and a ladies' car: the main distinction between which is that in the first, everybody smokes; and in the second, nobody does. As a black man never travels with a white one, there is also a negro car; which is a great blundering clumsy chest, such as Gulliver put to sea in, from the kingdom of Brobdignag. There is a great deal of jolting, a great deal of noise, a great deal of wall, not much window, a locomotive engine, a shriek, and a bell.

The cars are like shabby omnibuses, but larger: holding thirty, forty, fifty, people. The seats, instead of stretching from end to end, are placed crosswise. Each seat holds two persons. There is a long row of them on each side of the caravan, a narrow passage up the middle, and a door at both ends. In the centre of the carriage there is usually a stove, fed with charcoal or anthracite coal; which is for the most part red-hot. It is insufferably close; and you see the hot air fluttering between yourself and any other object you may happen to look at, like the ghost of smoke.

In the ladies' car, there are a great many gentlemen who have ladies with them. There are also a great many ladies who have nobody with them: for any lady may travel alone, from one end of the United States to the other, and be certain of the most courteous and considerate treatment everywhere. The conductor or check-taker, or guard, or whatever he may be, wears no uniform. He walks up and down the car, and in and out of it, as his fancy dictates; leans against the door with his hands in his pockets and stares at you, if you chance to be a stranger; or enters into conversation with the passengers about him. A great many newspapers are pulled out, and a few of them are read. Everybody talks to you, or to anybody else who hits his fancy. If you are an Englishman, he expects that that railroad is pretty much like an English railroad. If you say "No," he says "Yes?" (interrogatively), and asks in what respect they differ. You enumerate the heads of difference, one by one, and he says "Yes?" (still interrogatively) to each. Then he guesses that you don't travel faster in England; and on your replying that you do, says "Yes?" again (still interrogatively), and, it is quite evident, don't believe it. After a long pause he remarks, partly to you, and partly to the knob on the top of his stick, that "Yankees are reckoned to be considerable of a go-ahead people too"; upon which *you* say "Yes," and then *he* says "Yes" again (affirmatively this time); and upon your looking out of window, tells you that behind that hill, and some three miles from the next station, there is a clever town in a smart lo-ca-tion, where he expects you have con-cluded to stop. Your answer in the negative naturally leads to more questions in reference to your intended route (always pronounced rout); and wherever you are going, you invariably learn that you can't get there without immense difficulty and danger, and that all the great sights are somewhere else.

If a lady takes a fancy to any male passenger's seat, the gentleman who accompanies her gives him notice of the fact, and he immediately vacates it with great politeness. Politics are much discussed, so are banks, so is cotton. Quiet people avoid the question of the Presidency, for there will be a new election in three years and a half, and party feeling runs very high; the great constitutional feature of this institution being, that directly the acrimony of the last election is over, the acrimony of the next one begins; which is an unspeakable comfort to all strong politicians and true lovers of their country: that is to say, to ninety-nine men and boys out of every ninety-nine and a quarter.

Except when a branch road joins the main one, there is seldom more than one track of rails; so that the road is very narrow, and the view, where there is a deep cutting, by no means extensive. When there is not, the character of the scenery is always the same. Mile after mile of stunted trees: some hewn down by the axe, some blown down by the wind, some half fallen and resting on their neighbours, many mere logs half hidden in the swamp, others mouldered away to spongy chips. The very soil of the earth is made up of minute fragments such as these; each pool of stagnant water has its crust of vegetable rottenness; on every side there are the boughs, and trunks, and stumps of trees, in every possible stage of decay, decomposition, and neglect. Now you emerge for a few brief minutes on an open country, glittering with some bright lake or pool, broad as many an English river, but so small here that it scarcely has a name; now catch hasty glimpses of a distant town, with its clean white houses and their cool piazzas, its prim New England church and school-house; when whir-r-r-r! almost before you have seen them, comes the same dark screen; the stunted trees, the stumps, the logs, the stagnant water—all so like the last that you seem to have been transported back again by magic.

The train calls at stations in the woods, where the wild impossibility of anybody having the smallest reason to get out, is only to be equalled by the apparently desperate hopelessness of there being anybody to get in. It rushes across the turnpike road, where there is no gate, no policeman, no signal: nothing but a rough wooden arch, on which is painted "WHEN THE BELL RINGS, LOOK OUT FOR THE LOCO-MOTIVE." On it whirls headlong, dives through the woods again, emerges in the light, clatters over frail arches, rumbles upon the heavy ground, shoots beneath a wooden bridge which intercepts the light for a second like a wink, suddenly awakens all the slumbering echoes in the main street of a large town, and dashes on haphazard, pell-mell, neck-or-nothing, down the middle of the road. There—with

mechanics working at their trades, and people leaning from
their doors and windows, and boys flying kites and playing
marbles, and men smoking, and women talking, and children crawling, and pigs burrowing, and unaccustomed horses
plunging and rearing, close to the very rails—there—on,
on, on—tears the mad dragon of an engine with its train
of cars; scattering in all directions a shower of burning
sparks from its wood fire; screeching, hissing, yelling, panting; until at last the thirsty monster stops beneath a covered
way to drink, the people cluster round, and you have time
to breathe again.

CHARLES DICKENS

58. MR. PULLMAN'S FIRST CAR

MR. PULLMAN had an office on Madison Avenue just west of
LaSalle Street and I boarded with a family very close to his
office. I used to pass his office on my way to meals, and
having read in the paper that he was working on a sleeping
car, one day I stopped in and made application to Mr. Pullman
personally for a place as conductor. I gave him some references and called again and he said the references were alright
and promised me the place. I made my first trip between
Bloomington, Illinois, and Chicago on the night of September
1, 1859. I was twenty-two years old at the time. I wore no
uniform and was attired in citizen's clothes. I wore a badge,
that was all. One of my passengers was George M. Pullman,
inventor of the sleeping car. . . . All the passengers were from
Bloomington and there were no women on the car that night.
The people of Bloomington, little reckoning that history was
being made in their midst, did not come down to the station
to see the Pullman car's first trip. There was no crowd, and
the car, lighted by candles, moved away in solitary grandeur,
if such it might be called. . . . I remember on the first night I

had to compel the passengers to take their boots off before they got into the berths. They wanted to keep them on— seemed afraid to take them off.

J. L. BARNES

First Pullman Car Conductor in the United States

59. WELCOME, MASTER PULLMAN

[In 1875 George M. Pullman established a workshop at Turin, Italy. Here, under the direction of a Mr. A. Rapp, who was sent from the Detroit works, a number of Pullman cars were constructed for use on Italian expresses. The following testimonial was presented to Mr. Rapp at the conclusion of the work by the men who had been employed.]

TO

PULLMAN ESQUIRE, THE GREAT INVENTOR

OF THE

SALOON COMFORTABLE CARRIAGES

AND

MASTER RAPP THE CIVIL ENGINEER, DIRECTOR

OF THE MANUFACTURE OF THE SAME

THE

ITALIAN WORKMEN

BEG TO UMILIATE

Welcome, Welcome Master Pullman
The great inventor of the Saloon Carriages,
Italy will be thankful to the man
For now and ever, for ages and ages.

To Master Rapp we men are thankful.
Cause of his kindness and adviser sages,

Our hearts of true gladness is full:
And we shall remember him for ages.

Should Master Pullman ever succeed
To continue is work in Italy
What we wish to him indeed,
We hope to be chosen
To finish the work and work as a man,
To show our gratitude to Master Pullman.

FINO AND HIS FRIENDS

60. R. L. STEVENSON, EMIGRANT

IT was about two in the afternoon of Friday that I found myself in front of the Emigrant House, with more than a hundred others, to be sorted and boxed for the journey. A white-haired official, with a stick under one arm, and a list in the other hand, stood apart in front of us, and called name after name in the tone of a command. At each name you would see a family gather up its brats and bundles and run for the hindmost of the three cars that stood awaiting us, and I soon concluded that this was to be set apart for the women and children. The second or central car, it turned out, was devoted to men travelling alone, and the third to the Chinese. The official was easily moved to anger at the least delay; but the emigrants were both quick at answering their names, and speedy in getting themselves and their effects on board.

The families once housed, we men carried the second car without ceremony by simultaneous assault. I suppose the reader has some notion of an American railroad-car, that long, narrow wooden box, like a flat-roofed Noah's Ark, with a stove and a convenience, one at either end, a passage down the middle, and transverse benches upon either hand. Those destined for emigrants on the Union Pacific are only remarkable for their extreme plainness, nothing but wood entering in any part into their constitution, and for the usual inefficacy of the lamps, which often went out and shed but a dying glimmer even while they burned. The benches are too short for anything but a young child. Where there is scarce elbow-room for two to sit, there will not be space enough for one to lie. Hence the company, or rather, as it appears from certain bills about the Transfer Station, the company's servants, have conceived a plan for the better accommodation of travellers. They prevail on every two to chum together. To each of the chums they sell a board and three square cushions stuffed with straw, and covered with thin cotton. The benches can be made to face each other in pairs, for the backs are reversible. On the approach of night the boards are laid from bench to bench, making a couch wide enough for two, and long enough for a man of the middle height; and the chums lie down side by side upon the cushions with the head to the conductor's van and the feet to the engine. When the train is full, of course this plan is impossible, for there must not be more than one to every bench, neither can it be carried out unless the chums agree. It was to bring about this last condition that our white-haired official now bestirred himself. He made a most active master of ceremonies, introducing likely couples, and even guaranteeing the amiability and honesty of each. The greater the number of happy couples the better for his pocket, for it was he who sold the raw material of the beds. His price for one board and three straw cushions began with two dollars and a half; but before the train left, and, I am sorry to say, long after I had purchased mine, it had fallen to one dollar and a half.

The match-maker had a difficulty with me; perhaps, like some ladies, I showed myself too eager for union at any price, but certainly the first who was picked out to be my bedfellow, declined the honour without thanks. He was an old, heavy slow-spoken man, I think from Yankeeland, looked me all over with great timidity, and then began to excuse himself in broken phrases. He didn't know the young man, he said. The young man might be very honest, but how was he to know that? There was another young man whom he had met already in the train; he guessed *he* was honest, and would prefer to chum with *him* upon the whole. All this without any sort of excuse, as though I had been inanimate or absent. I began to tremble lest every one should refuse my company, and I be left rejected. But the next in turn was a tall, strapping, long-limbed, small-headed, curly-haired Pennsylvania Dutchman, with a soldierly smartness in his manner. To be exact, he had acquired it in the navy. But that was all one; he had at least been trained to desperate resolves, so he accepted the match, and the white-haired swindler pronounced the connubial benediction, and pocketed his fees.

The rest of the afternoon was spent in making up the train. I am afraid to say how many baggage-waggons followed the engine, certainly a score; then came the Chinese, then we, then the families, and the rear was brought up by the conductor, in what, if I have it rightly, is called his caboose. The class to which I belonged was of course far the largest, and we ran over, so to speak to both sides; so that there were some Caucasians among the Chinamen, and some bachelors among the families. But our own car was pure from admixture, save for one little boy of eight or nine who had the whooping-cough. At last, about six, the long train crawled out of the Transfer Station and across the wide Missouri river to Omaha, westward bound.

It was a troubled uncomfortable evening in the cars. There was thunder in the air, which helped to keep us restless. A man played many airs upon the cornet, and none of them were much attended to, until he came to "Home, sweet home." It was truly strange to note how the talk ceased at that, and the faces began to lengthen. . . .

The day faded; the lamps were lit; a party of wild young men, who got off next evening at North Platte, stood together on the stern platform, singing "The Sweet By-and-bye" with very tuneful voices; the chums began to put up their beds, and it seemed as if the business of the day were at an end. But it was not so; for, the train stopping at some station, the cars were instantly thronged with the natives, wives and fathers, young men and maidens, some of them in little more than nightgear, some with stable lanterns, and all offering beds for sale. Their charge began with twenty-five cents a cushion, but fell, before the train went on again, to fifteen, with the bed-board gratis, or less than one-fifth of what I had paid for mine at the Transfer. This is my contribution to the economy of future emigrants.

A great personage on an American train is the newsboy. He sells books (such books!), papers, fruit, lollipops, and cigars; and on emigrant journeys, soap, towels, tin washing dishes, tin coffee pitchers, coffee, tea, sugar, and tinned eatables, mostly hash or beans and bacon. Early next morning the newsboy went around the cars, and chumming on a more extended principle became the order of the hour. It requires but a copartnery of two to manage beds; but washing and eating can be carried on most economically by a syndicate of three. I myself entered a little after sunrise into articles of agreement, and became one of the firm of Pennsylvania, Shakespeare, and Dubuque, the name of a place in the State of Iowa, that of an amiable young fellow going west to cure an asthma, and retarding his recovery by incessantly chewing or smoking, and sometimes chewing and smoking together. I have never seen tobacco so sillily abused. Shakespeare bought a tin washing-dish, Dubuque a towel, and Pennsylvania a brick of soap. The partners used these instruments, one after another, according to the order of their first awaking; and when the firm had finished there was no want of borrowers. Each filled the tin dish at the water filter opposite the stove, and retired with the whole stock in trade to the platform of the car. There he knelt down, supporting himself by a shoulder against the woodwork or one elbow crooked about the railing, and made a shift to wash his face and neck and hands; a cold, an insufficient, and, if the train is moving rapidly, a somewhat dangerous toilet.

On a similar division of expense, the firm of Pennsylvania, Shakespeare, and Dubuque supplied themselves with coffee, sugar, and necessary vessels; and their operations are a type of what went on through all the cars. Before the sun was up the stove would be brightly burning; at the first station the natives would come on board with milk and eggs and coffee cakes; and soon from end to end the car would be filled with little parties breakfasting upon the bed-boards. It was the pleasantest hour of the day.

There were meals to be had, however, by the wayside: a breakfast in the morning, a dinner somewhere between eleven and two, and supper from five to eight or nine at night. We had rarely less than twenty minutes for each; and if we had not spent many another twenty minutes waiting for some express upon a side track among the miles of desert, we might have taken an hour to each repast and arrived at San Francisco up to time. For haste is not the foible of an emigrant train. It gets through on sufferance, running the gauntlet among its more considerable brethren; should there be a block, it is unhesitatingly sacrificed; and they cannot, in consequence, predict the length of the passage within a day or so. Civility is the main comfort that you miss. Equality, though conceived very largely in America, does not extend so low down as to an emigrant. Thus in all other trains, a warning cry of "All aboard!" recalls the passengers to take their seats; but as soon as I was alone with emigrants, and from the Transfer all the way to San Francisco, I found this ceremony was pretermitted; the train stole from the station without note of warning, and you had to keep an eye upon it even while you ate. . . .

It had thundered on the Friday night, but the sun rose on Saturday without a cloud. We were at sea—there is no other adequate expression—on the plains of Nebraska. I made my observatory on the top of a fruit-waggon, and sat by the hour upon that perch to spy about me, and to spy in vain for something new. It was a world almost without a feature; an empty sky, an empty earth; front and back, the line of railway stretched from horizon to horizon, like a cue across a billiard-board; on either hand, the green plain ran till it touched the skirts of heaven. Along the track innumerable wild sunflowers, no bigger than a crown-piece, bloomed in a continuous flower-bed; grazing beasts were seen upon the prairie at all degrees of distance and diminution; and now and again we might perceive a few dots beside the railroad which grew more and more distinct as we drew nearer till they turned into wooden cabins, and then dwindled and dwindled in our wake until they melted into their surroundings, and we were once more alone upon the billiard-board. The train toiled over this infinity like a snail; and being the one thing moving, it was wonderful what huge proportions it began to assume in our regard. It seemed miles in length, and either end of it within but a step of the horizon. Even my own body or my own head seemed a great thing in that emptiness. I note the feeling the more readily as it is the contrary of what I have read of in the experience of others. Day and night, above the roar of the train, our ears were kept busy with the incessant chirp of grasshoppers—a noise like the winding up of countless clocks and watches, which began after a while to seem proper to that land. . . .

I had been suffering in my health a good deal all the way; and at last, whether I was exhausted by my complaint or poisoned in some wayside eating-house, the evening we left Laramie, I fell sick outright. That was a night which I shall not readily forget. The lamps did not go out; each made a faint shining in its own neighbourhood, and the shadows were confounded together in the long, hollow box of the car. The sleepers lay in uneasy attitudes; here two chums alongside, flat upon their backs like dead folk; there a man sprawling on the floor, with his face upon his arm; there another half seated with his head and shoulders on the bench. The most passive were continually and roughly shaken by the movement of the train; others stirred, turned, or stretched out their arms like children; it was surprising how many groaned and murmured in their sleep; and as I passed to and fro, stepping across the prostrate, and caught now a snore, now a gasp, now a half-formed word, it gave me a measure of the worthlessness of rest in that unresting vehicle. Although it was chill, I was obliged to open my window, for the degradation of the air soon became intolerable to one who was awake and using the full supply of life. Outside, in a glimmering night, I saw the black, amorphous hills shoot by unweariedly into our wake. They that long for morning have never longed for it more earnestly than I.

And yet when day came, it was to shine upon the same unbroken and unsightly quarter of the world. Mile upon mile, and not a tree, a bird, or a river. Only down the long, sterile cañons, the train shot hooting and awoke the resting echo. That train was the one piece of life in all the deadly land; it was the one actor, the one spectacle fit to be observed in this paralysis of man and nature. And when I think how the railroad has been pushed through this unwatered wilderness and haunt of savage tribes, and now will bear an emigrant for some £12 from the Atlantic to the Golden Gates; how at each stage of the construction, roaring, impromptu cities, full of gold and lust and death, sprang up and then died away again, and are now but wayside stations in the desert; how in these uncouth places pig-tailed Chinese pirates worked side by side with border ruffians and broken men from Europe, talking together in a mixed dialect, mostly oaths, gambling, drinking, quarrelling and murdering like wolves; how the plumed hereditary lord of all America heard, in this last fastness, the scream of the "bad medicine waggon" charioting his foes; and then when I go on to remember that all this epical turmoil was conducted by gentlemen in frock coats, and with a view to nothing more extraordinary than a fortune and a subsequent visit to Paris, it seems to me, I own, as if this railway were the one typical achievement of the age in which we live, as if it brought together into one plot all the ends of the world and all the degrees of social rank, and offered to some great writer the busiest, the most extended, and the most varied subject for an enduring literary work. If it be romance, if it be contrast, if it be heroism that we require, what was Troy town to this? But, alas! it is not these things that are necessary—it is only Homer. . .

ROBERT LOUIS STEVENSON

61. RIDING THE RODS

BRUM informed me of a freight train that was to leave the yards at midnight, on which we could beat our way to a small town on the borders of the hop country. Not knowing what to do with ourselves until that time arrived, we continued to drink until we were not in a fit condition for this hazardous undertaking—except we were fortunate to get an empty car, so as to lie down and sleep upon the journey. At last we made our way towards the yards, where we saw the men making up the train. We kept out of sight until that was done and then in the darkness Brum inspected one side of the train and I the other, in quest of an empty car. In vain we sought for that comfort. There was nothing to do but to ride the bumpers or the top of the car, exposed to the cold night air. We jumped the bumpers, the engine whistled twice, toot! toot! and we felt ourselves slowly moving out of the yards. Brum was on one car and I was on the next facing him. Never shall I forget the horrors of that ride. He had taken fast hold on the handle bar of his car, and I had done likewise with mine. We had been riding some fifteen minutes, and the train was going at its full speed when, to my horror, I saw Brum lurch forward, and then quickly pull himself straight and erect. Several times he did this, and I shouted to him. It was no use, for the man was drunk and fighting against the over-powering effects, and it was a mystery to me how he kept his hold. At last he became motionless for so long that I knew the next time he lurched forward his weight of body must break his hold, and he would fall under the wheels and be cut to pieces. I worked myself carefully towards him and woke him. Although I had great difficulty in waking him, he swore that he was not asleep. I had scarcely done this when a lantern was shown from the top of the car, and a brakesman's voice hailed us. "Hallo, where are you two going?" "To the hop fields," I answered. "Well," he sneered, "I guess you won't get to them on this train, so jump off, at once. Jump! d'ye hear?" he cried, using a great oath, as he saw we were little inclined to obey. Brum was now wide awake. "If you don't jump at once," shouted this irate brakesman, "you will be thrown off." "To jump," said Brum quietly, "will be sure death, and to be thrown off will mean no more." "Wait until I come back," cried the brakesman, "and we will see whether you ride this train or not," on which he left us, making his way towards the caboose.

"Now," said Brum, "when he returns we must be on the top of the car, for he will probably bring with him a coupling pin to strike us off the bumpers, making us fall under the wheels." We quickly clambered on top and in a few minutes could see a light approaching us, moving along the top of the cars. We were now lying flat, so that he might not see us until he stood on the same car. He was very near to us, when we sprang to our feet, and unexpectedly gripped him, one on each side, and before he could recover from his first astonishment. In all my life I have never seen so much fear on a human face. He must have seen our half drunken condition and at once gave up all hopes of mercy from such men, for he stood helpless, not knowing what to do. If he struggled it would mean the fall and death of the three, and did he remain helpless in our hands, it might mean being thrown from that height from a car going at the rate of thirty miles an hour. "Now," said Brum to him, "what is it to be? Shall we ride this train without interference, or shall we have a wrestling bout up here, when the first fall must be our last? Speak!" "Boys," said he, affecting a short laugh, "you have the drop on me; you can ride." We watched him making his way back to the caboose, which he entered, but every moment I expected to see him reappear assisted by others. It might have been that there was some friction among them, and that they would not ask assistance from one another. For instance, an engineer has to take orders from the conductor, but the former is as well paid, if not better, than the latter, and the most responsibility is on his shoulders, and this often makes ill blood between them. At any rate, American tramps know well that neither the engineer nor the fireman, his faithful attendant, will inform the conductor or brakesman of their presence on a train. Perhaps the man was ashamed of his ill-success, and did not care to own his defeat to the conductor and his fellow brakesmen; but whatever was the matter, we rode that train to its destination and without any more interference.

W. H. DAVIES

62. SPEEDS IN BRAZIL AND PERU

WE have not had very accurate figures to work with, but we believe that no trains attain 29 miles per hour inclusive in either country: so that here at least Mr. Ruskin or Ouida might live a contented life.

E. FOXWELL AND T. C. FARRER

A Chapter of Accidents

TRAIN SNOWED UP NEAR DENT, 1881

63. DREADFUL ACCIDENT
TO MR. HUSKISSON

(From our own Correspondent)

LIVERPOOL, half-past 8 o'clock, Wednesday night.

I HAVE just returned from our journey along the rail-road
from Liverpool to Manchester, and back again; and although
I had intended to give you some faint description of this
astounding work of art, of the crowds which lined almost
every inch of our road, of the flags and banners, and booths
and scaffoldings, and gorgeous tents, which have enlivened
even the dullest parts of our journey, I am obliged, on account
of the lateness of the hour, to defer that description as comparatively uninteresting, owing to the fatal accident that has
befallen Mr. Huskisson . . .

Mr. Huskisson was discoursing with Mr. Joseph Sandars,
one of the principal originators and promoters of this railroad, and was congratulating that gentleman as one of the
happiest men in the world, in having seen a work of such
importance and magnitude happily brought to a conclusion
under his auspices, when he was called away to speak with
some other gentlemen, who were anxious to hear his opinion
on some of the details of the road. Before he left Mr. Sandars,

he said to that gentleman, "Well, I must go and shake hands with the Duke[1] on this day at any rate." The gentlemen who had called him away detained him some time, and whilst he was standing with them, the *Rocket* engine, which, like the *Phoenix*, had to pass the Duke's car, to take up its station at the watering place, came slowly up, and as the engineer had been for some time checking its velocity, so silently that it was almost upon the group before they observed it. In the hurry of the moment all attempted to get out of the way. Mr. Holmes M.P. who was standing by the side of Mr. Huskisson, desired the gentlemen not to stir, but to cling close by the side of their own car—most excellent advice, had it been followed—for as no engine can move off the rail, any person who stands clear of it, is perfectly safe from danger. Unfortunately, in the hurry and agitation of the moment, Mr. Huskisson did not pursue this advice. He hesitated, staggered a little as if not knowing what to do, then attempted to run forward, found it impossible to get off the road, on account of an excavation of some 14 or 15 feet depth being on that side of it on which he was, attempted again to get into the car, was hit by a motion of the door as he was mounting a step, and was thrown down directly in the path of the *Rocket*, as that engine came opposite to the Duke's car. He contrived to move himself a little out of its path before it came in contact with him, otherwise it must have gone directly over his head and breast. As it was, the wheel went over his left thigh, squeezing it almost to a jelly, broke the leg, it is said, in two places, laid the muscles bare from the ankle nearly to the hip, and tore out a large piece of flesh as it left him. Mrs. Huskisson, who, along with several other ladies, witnessed the accident, uttered a shriek of agony, which none who heard will ever forget. As soon as Mr.

---

[1] Wellington, with whom at that time Huskisson was on bad terms.

Huskisson could be raised from the ground, he asked where Mrs. Huskisson was, and in the most cool and collected manner gave such directions as he thought best fitted for the situation in which he was placed. Mrs. Huskisson was immediately by his side to attend to his wishes, but was soon obliged to give way to Dr. Brandreth, who applied a tourniquet to stop the dreadful effusion of blood under which Mr. Huskisson was suffering. In a few minutes afterwards Mr. Huskisson fainted away, and in that condition was removed, as carefully as circumstances would allow, into the car, in which the band of music preceding the Duke's car had been placed. The musicians were immediately turned out of it, and Mrs. Huskisson, Mr. Wainewright (Mr. Huskisson's private secretary), and several other of Mr. Huskisson's friends took their places. The Duke's car was detached from the *Northumbrian* engine and fastened laterally to the two engines *Phoenix* and *North Star*. The *Northumbrian* engine then having no other weight to draw but the car which had carried the band, and was now occupied by Mr. Huskisson and his party, proceeded at a rapid rate to Manchester to procure medical assistance. As it passed by our car Mr. Huskisson was laid at the bottom of it, pale and ghostly as death, and his wife was hanging over him in an agony of tears.

THE TIMES, Friday, 17 September 1830

64. A QUICK DECISION

THE elder Brunel[1] was habitually absent in society, but no man was more remarkable for presence of mind in an emergency. Numerous instances are recorded of this latter quality, but none more striking than that of his adventure in the act of inspecting the Birmingham Railway. Suddenly in a confined part of the road a train was seen approaching from either

[1] Sir Marc Brunel; Isambard's father.

end of the line, and at a speed which it was difficult to calculate. The spectators were horrified; there was not an instant to be lost; but an instant sufficed to the experienced engineer to determine the safest course under the circumstances. Without attempting to cross the road, which would have been almost certain destruction, he at once took his position exactly midway between the up and down lines, and drawing the skirts of his coat close around him, allowed the two trains to sweep past him; when to the great relief of those who witnessed the exciting scene, he was found untouched upon the road. Without the engineer's experience which enabled him to form so rapid a decision, there can be no doubt that he must have perished.

RALPH AND CHANDOS TEMPLE

65. FIRE!

ON the 8th of December I left Darlington by the 9h. 25m. train for London. I travelled in my chariot with my maid. The carriage was strapped on to a truck and placed with its back to the engine, about the centre of the train, which was a long one. Soon after leaving Leicester I thought I smelt something burning and told my maid to look out of the window on her side to see if anything was on fire. She let down the window, and so many lumps of red-hot coal or coke were showering down that she put it up again immediately. I still thought I smelt something burning; she put down the window again and exclaimed that the carriage was on fire. We then put down the side-windows and waved our handkerchiefs, screaming "fire" as loud as we could. No one took any notice of us. I then pulled up the windows, lest the current of air through the carriage should cause the fire to burn more rapidly into the carriage, and determined to sit in as long as possible. After some time, seeing that no assistance was likely to be afforded us, my maid became terrified, and without telling me her intention, opened the door, let down the step, and scrambled out on to the truck. I followed her, but having unluckily let myself down towards the back part of the carriage, which was on fire, was obliged to put up the step and close the door as well as I could to enable me to pass to the front part of the carriage, furthest from the fire, and where my maid was standing. We clung on by the front springs of the carriage, screaming "fire" incessantly, and waving our handkerchiefs. We passed several policemen on the road, none of whom took any notice of us. No guard appeared. A gentleman in the carriage behind mine saw us, but could render no assistance. My maid seemed in an agony of terror, and I saw her sit down on the side of the truck and gather her cloak tightly about her. I think I told her to hold fast to the carriage. I turned away for a moment to wave my handkerchief, and when I looked round again my poor maid was gone. The train went on, the fire of course increasing, and the wind blowing it towards me. A man (a passenger) crept along the ledge of the railway carriages and came as near as possible to the truck on which I stood, but it was impossible for him to help me. At last the train stopped at the Rugby station. An engine was sent back to find my maid. She was found on the road and taken to Leicester hospital, where she now lies in an almost hopeless state; her skull fractured; three of her fingers have been amputated. I am told the train was going at the rate of 50 miles an hour.

THE COUNTESS OF ZETLAND

66. UNFAMILIARITY BREEDS CONTEMPT

NEITHER the companies' servants nor the public had yet learned to treat railway trains with the necessary caution. Engine-drivers fancied that a collision between two engines was much the same thing as the inter-locking of the wheels of two rival stage-coaches. Passengers tried to jump on and off trains moving at full speed with absolute recklessness. Again and again is it recorded, "injured, jumped out after his hat"; "fell off, riding on the side of a wagon"; "skull broken, riding on the top of the carriage, came in collision with a bridge"; "guard's head struck against a bridge, attempting to remove a passenger who had improperly seated himself outside"; "fell out of a third-class carriage while pushing and jostling with a friend." "Of the serious accidents reported to the Board of Trade," writes one authority, "twenty-two happened to persons who jumped off when the carriages were going at speed, generally after their hats, and five persons were run over when lying either drunk or asleep upon the line."

W. M. ACWORTH

67. LET THE BURNT BISHOP...

[On May 8, 1842, an accident occurred between Versailles and Paris in which 52 lives were lost. Many of the victims were burnt to death owing to the practice of locking the carriage doors. The incident spread alarm among travellers on the Great Western, where the same practice was current, and caused Sydney Smith to address the Editor of the *Morning Chronicle*.]

7 June, 1842

SIR,

Since the letter upon railroads, which you were good enough to insert in your paper, I have had some conversation with two gentlemen officially connected with the Great Western. Though nothing could be more courteous than their manner, nor more intelligible than their arguments, I remain unshaken as to the necessity of keeping the doors open.

There is, in the first place, the effect of imagination, the idea that all escape is impossible, that (let what will happen) you must sit quiet in first class No. 2, whether they are pounding you into jam, or burning you into a cinder, or crumbling you into a human powder. These excellent directors, versant in wood and metal, seem to require that the imagination should be sent by some other conveyance, and that only loads of unimpassioned, unintellectual flesh and blood should be darted along on the Western rail; whereas, the female *homo* is a screaming, parturient, interjectional, hysterical animal, whose delicacy and timidity, monopolists even (much as it may surprise them) must be taught to consult. The female, in all probability, never would jump out; but she thinks she may jump out when she pleases; and this is intensely comfortable. . . .

The truth is—and so (after a hundred monopolizing experiments on public patience) the railroad directors will find it—there can be no other dependence for the safety of the public than the care which every human being is inclined to take of his own life and limbs. Every thing beyond this is the mere lazy tyranny of monopoly, which makes no distinction between human beings and brown paper parcels. If riding were a monopoly, as travelling in carriages is now become, there are many gentlemen whom I see riding in the Park upon such false principles, that I am sure the cantering and galloping directors would strap them, in the ardour of their affection, to the saddle, padlock them to the stirrups, or compel them to ride behind a policeman of the stable; and nothing but a motion from O'Brian, or an order from Gladstone, could release them. . . .

But the most absurd of all legislative enactments is this hemiplegian law—an act of Parliament to protect one side of the body and not the other. If the wheel comes off on the right, the open door is uppermost, and every one is saved. If, from any sudden avalanche on the road, the carriage is prostrated to the left, the locked door is uppermost, all escape is impossible, and the rail-road martyrdom begins.

Leave me to escape in the best way I can, as the fire-offices very kindly permit me to do. I know very well the danger of getting out on the off-side; but escape is the affair of a moment; suppose a train to have passed at that moment, I know I am safe from any other trains for twenty minutes or half an hour; and if I do get out on the off-side, I do not remain in the valley of death between the two trains, but am over to the opposite bank in an instant—only half-roasted, or merely browned, certainly not done enough for the Great Western directors. . . .

Railroad travelling is a delightful improvement of human life. Man is become a bird; he can fly longer and quicker than a Solan goose. The mamma rushes sixty miles in two hours to the aching finger of her conjugating and declining grammar boy. The early Scotchman scratches himself in the morning mists of the North, and has his porridge in Piccadilly before the setting sun. The Puseyite priest, after a rush of 100 miles, appears with his little volume of nonsense at the breakfast of his bookseller. Everything is near, everything is immediate—time, distance, and delay are abolished. But, though charming and fascinating as all this is, we must not shut our eyes to the price we shall pay for it. There will be every three or four years some dreadful massacre—whole trains will be hurled down a precipice, and 200 or 300 persons will be killed on the spot. There will be every now and then a great combustion of human bodies, as there has been at Paris; then all the newspapers up in arms—a thousand regulations, forgotten as soon as the directors dare—loud screams of the velocity whistle—monopoly locks and bolts, as before.

We have been, up to this point, very careless of our railway regulations. The first person of rank who is killed will put everything in order, and produce a code of the most careful rules. I hope it will not be one of the bench of bishops; but should it be so destined, let the burnt bishop—the unwilling Latimer—remember that, however painful gradual concoction by fire may be, his death will produce unspeakable benefit to the public. Even Sodor and Man will be better than nothing. From that moment, the bad effects of the monopoly are destroyed; no more fatal deference to the directors; no despotic incarceration, no barbarous inattention to the anatomy and physiology of the human body; no commitment to locomotive prisons with warrant. We shall then find it possible "Voyager libre sans mourir."

I am, Sir, your obedient servant,

SYDNEY SMITH

68. LOST PROPERTY

Bubworth, Nr. Retford, July 16, 1842

SIR,

A Bull was sent last Tuesday to the Eckington Station and placed on the train which passes there at eleven o'clock to be conveyed to the Wolverton Station. He had a direction on parchment tied round his neck to Mr. Anderson at H. C. Hoare Esqre, Wovendon House, Nr. Newport Pagnell, Bucks, and it was written legibly thereon that he was to be left at the Wolverton Station—he has I am sorry to say not been heard of there. Will you be so good as to forward him as directed if he is remaining at Euston Square.

I am very much surprised how any mistake can have arisen as I had previously written to the Manager at the Eckington Station stating where he would have to be left.

I am, Sir, Your obedient Servant,

WM. BROOKE

An answer would greatly oblige.

69. ACCIDENT OF BIRTH

LORD FREDERIC HAMILTON records a story of the Indian Census of 1891, when a man gave his place of birth as "a first-class carriage on the London and North-Western Railway, somewhere between Bletchley and Euston; the precise spot being unnoticed either by myself or the other person principally concerned."

70. ABERGELE

IT occurred in 1868, and to the "Irish mail," perhaps the most famous train which is run in England, if, indeed, not in the world. Leaving London shortly after 7 A.M., the Irish mail was then timed to make the distance to Chester, 166 miles, in four hours and eighteen minutes, or at the rate of 40 miles an hour. For the next 85 miles, completing the run to Holyhead, the speed was somewhat increased, two hours and five minutes being allowed for it. Abergele is a point on the sea-coast of Wales, nearly midway between Chester and Holyhead. On the day of the accident, August 20, 1868, the Irish mail left Chester as usual. It was made up of thirteen carriages in all, which were occupied, as the carriages of that train usually were, by a large number of persons whose names at least were widely known. Among these, on this particular occasion, was the Duchess of Abercorn, wife of the then Lord Lieutenant of Ireland, with five children. Under the running arrangements of the London & North Western road a freight, or as it is called a goods train, left Chester half an hour before the mail, and was placed upon the siding at Llanddulas, a station about a mile and a half beyond Abergele, to allow the mail to pass. From Abergele to Llanddulas the track ascended by a gradient of some sixty feet to the mile. On the day of the accident it chanced that certain wagons between the engine and the rear end of the goods train had to be taken out to be left at Llanddulas, and in doing this it became necessary to separate the train and to leave five or six of the last wagons in it standing on the tracks of the main line, while those which were to be left were backed on to a siding. The employé, whose duty it was, neglected to set the brakes on the wagons thus left standing, and consequently when the engine and the rest of the train returned for them, the moment they were touched and before a coupling could be effected, the jar set them in motion down the incline towards Abergele. They started so slowly that a brakesman of the train ran after them, fully expecting to catch and stop them, but as they went down the grade they soon out-stripped him and it became clear that there was nothing to check them until they should meet the Irish mail, then almost due. It also chanced that the cars thus set in motion were oil cars.

The track of the North Western road between Abergele and Llanddulas runs along the sides of the picturesque Welsh hills, which rise up to the south, while to the north there stretches out a wide expanse of sea. The mail train was skirting the hills and labouring up the grade at a speed of thirty miles an hour, when its engineer suddenly became aware of the loose wagons coming down upon it around the curve, and then but a few yards off. Seeing that they were oil cars he almost instinctively sprang from his locomotive, and was thrown down by the impetus and rolled to the side of the road-bed. Picking himself up, bruised but not seriously hurt, he saw that the collision had already taken place, that the tender had ridden directly over the engine, that the colliding cars were demolished, and that the foremost carriages of the train were already on fire. Running quickly to the rear of the train he succeeded in uncoupling six carriages and a van, which were drawn away from the rest, before the flames extended to them, by an engine which most fortunately was following the train. All the other carriages were utterly destroyed, and every person in them perished.

The most graphic description of this extraordinary and terrible catastrophe was that given by the Marquis of Hamilton, the eldest son of the Duke of Abercorn whose wife and family, fortunately for themselves, occupied one of those rear carriages which were unshackled and saved. In this account the Marquis of Hamilton said: "We were startled by a collision and a shock which, though not very severe, were sufficient to throw every one against his opposite neighbor. I immediately jumped out of the carriage, when a fearful sight met my view. Already the whole of the three passengers' carriages in front of ours, the vans, and the engine were enveloped in dense sheets of flame and smoke, rising fully twenty feet high, and spreading out in every direction. It was the work of an instant. No words can convey the instantaneous nature of the explosion and conflagration. I had actually got out almost before the shock of the collision was over, and this was the spectacle which already presented itself. Not a sound, not a scream, not a struggle to escape, not a movement of any sort was apparent in the doomed carriages. It was as though an electric flash had at once paralysed and stricken every one of their occupants. So complete was the absence of any presence of living or struggling life in them that as soon as the passengers from the other parts of the train were in some degree recovered from their first shock and consternation, it was imagined that the burning carriages were destitute of passengers; a hope soon changed into feelings of horror when their contents of charred and mutilated remains were discovered an hour afterward."

C. F. ADAMS

71. LEAP BEFORE YOU LOOK

MANY concussions give no warning of their approach, while others do, the usual premonitory symptoms being a kind of bouncing or leaping of the train. It is well to know that the bottom of the carriage is the safest place, and, therefore, when a person has reason to anticipate a concussion, he should, without hesitation, throw himself on the floor of the carriage. It was by this means that Lord Guillamore saved his life and that of his fellow passengers some years since, when a concussion took place on one of the Irish railways. His Lordship feeling a shock, which he knew to be the forerunner of a concussion, without more ado sprang upon the two persons sitting opposite to him, and dragged them with him to the bottom of the carriage; the astonished persons first imagined that they had been set upon by a maniac, and commenced struggling for their liberty, but in a few seconds they but too well understood the nature of the case; the concussion came, and the upper part of the carriage in which Lord Guillamore and the other two persons were was shattered to pieces, while the floor was untouched, and thus left them lying in safety; while the other carriages of the train presented nothing but a ghastly spectacle of dead and wounded.

THE RAILWAY TRAVELLER'S HANDY BOOK

72. DRIVER LEGGE

DRIVER LEGGE was blown up with his boiler. His arms and legs were hurled in different directions, and one of the former actually went through the window of a private house and fell upon a breakfast-table round which the family were sitting at the time.

MICHAEL REYNOLDS

73. BALLOON ON THE LINE

YESTERDAY evening, Aug. 6th, 1883, a special train of "empties," which left Charing Cross at 5.55 to pick up returning excursionists from Gravesend, had some extraordinary experiences, such as perhaps had hardly ever occurred on a single journey. On leaving Dartford, where some passengers were taken up, the train was proceeding towards Greenhithe, when the driver observed on the line a donkey, which had strayed from an adjoining field. An endeavour was made to stop the train before the animal was reached, but without success, and the poor beast was knocked down and dragged along by the firebox of the engine. The train was stopped, and with great difficulty the body of the animal, which was killed, was extricated from beneath the engine. While this was in progress, a balloon called the "Sunbeam," supposed to come either from Sydenham or Tunbridge Wells, passed over the line, going in the direction of Northfleet. The two aeronauts in the car were observed to be short of gas, and were throwing out ballast, but, notwithstanding this, the balloon descended slowly, and when some distance ahead of the train was, to the horror of the passengers, seen to drop suddenly into the railway cutting two or three hundred yards ahead only in advance of the approaching train. The alarm whistle was sounded, and the brakes put on, and as the balloon dragged the car and its occupants over the down line there seemed nothing but certain death for them; but suddenly the inflated monster, now swaying about wildly, took a sudden upward flight, and, dragging the car clear of the line, fell into an adjoining field just when the train was within a hundred yards of the spot. The escape was marvellous.

ANON

74. THE COMPANY'S RULES

"ACCIDENT" seems to be so much an admitted matter of course in railway travelling that we presume we must pass over the sudden stoppage of a passenger train at a distance of two miles from a station for no other apparent purpose than to give time for a luggage train to come up and run into it. There seems to have been something wrong in the engine which occasioned the halt and rendered it incumbent on the deceased engine-driver to alight that he might execute some repairs; but even this incident would not have exposed the train to a collision had the 20 minutes that elapsed been made use of to prevent the accident. Instead of this being done, the time was consumed in a perfectly cool and deliberate, but utterly fruitless, attempt to work out the rules of the company, which were intended to be applicable in cases of danger. The guard, with creditable promptitude, began to execute what he believed to be his duty, according to the rules; and though they directed him undoubtedly to be in two places at a time, and perform some three or four operations at once, he declined putting upon them their widest construction, but preferred limiting their sense by a reference to human capability. [As for the second train] the engineman is told merely to keep a sharp look-out forward . . . but the stoker or fire-man is distinctly ordered to look out forwards and backwards —in the former case with sharpness, and in the latter with frequency. How he is to accomplish this double duty of keeping his eyes vigilantly employed in two opposite directions we are not aware. . . .

THE TIMES, 17 February, 1848

75. SMASH AT STAPLEHURST

Gad's Hill Place, Higham by Rochester, Kent.
Tuesday, Thirteenth June, 1865.

My dear Mitton,

I should have written to you yesterday or the day before, if I had been quite up to writing.

I was in the only carriage that did not go over into the stream. It was caught upon the turn by some of the ruin of the bridge, and hung suspended and balanced in an apparently impossible manner. Two ladies were my fellow-passengers, an old one and a young one. This is exactly what passed. You may judge from it the precise length of the suspense. Suddenly we were off the rail, and beating the ground as the car of a half-emptied balloon might. The old lady cried out "My God!" and the young one screamed. I caught hold of them both (the old lady sat opposite and the young one on my left) and said: "We can't help ourselves, but we can be quiet and composed. Pray don't cry out." The old lady immediately answered: "Thank you. Rely upon me. Upon my soul I will be quiet." We were then all tilted down together in a corner of the carriage, and stopped. I said to them thereupon, "You may be sure nothing worse can happen. Our danger *must* be over. Will you remain here without stirring, while I get out of the window?" They both answered quite collectedly "Yes" and I got out without the least notion what had happened.

Fortunately I got out with great caution and stood upon the step. Looking down I saw the bridge gone, and nothing below me but the line of rail. Some people in the two other compartments were madly trying to plunge out of the window, and had no idea that there was an open swampy field fifteen feet down below them, and nothing else! The two guards (one with his face cut) were running up and down on the down side of the bridge (which was not torn up) quite wildly. I called out to them: "Look at me. Do stop an instant and look at me, and tell me whether you don't know me." One of them answered, "We know you very well, Mr. Dickens." "Then," I said, "my good fellow, for God's sake give me your key, and send one of those labourers here, and I'll empty this carriage." We did it quite safely, by means of a plank or two, and when it was done I saw all the rest of the train, except the two baggage vans, down in the stream. I got into the carriage again for my brandy flask, took off my travelling hat for a basin, climbed down the brickwork, and filled my hat with water.

Suddenly I came upon a staggering man covered with blood (I think he must have been flung clean out of his carriage), with such a frightful cut across the skull that I couldn't bear to look at him. I poured some water over his face and gave him some drink, then gave him some brandy, and laid him down on the grass, and he said: "I am gone," and died afterwards. Then I stumbled over a lady lying on her back against a little pollard-tree, with the blood streaming over her face (which was lead colour) in a number of distinct little streams from the head. I asked her if she could swallow a little brandy and she just nodded, and I gave her some and left her for somebody else. The next time I passed her she was dead. Then a man, examined at the inquest yesterday (who evidently had not the least remembrance of what really passed), came running up to me and implored me to help him find his wife, who was afterwards found dead. No imagination can conceive the ruin of the carriages, or the extraordinary weights under which the people were lying, or the complications into which they were twisted up among iron and wood, and mud and water.

I don't want to be examined at the inquest and I don't want to write about it. I could do no good either way, and I could only seem to speak about myself, which of course I would rather not do. I am keeping very quiet here. I have a —I don't know what to call it—constitutional (I suppose) presence of mind, and was not in the least fluttered at the time. I instantly remembered that I had the MS. of a number with me and clambered back into the carriage for it. But in writing these scanty words of recollection I feel the shake and am obliged to stop.

Ever faithfully,

CHARLES DICKENS

76. CELTIC TWILIGHT

THE Ulster Company availed themselves of the recommendation of the Irish Railway Commissioners, and completed twenty-five miles of the way from Belfast to Dublin on the six feet two inches scale; while the Drogheda Company, which set out from Dublin to meet the Ulster line, adopted a gauge of five feet two inches. When this discrepancy was complained of by the Directors of the Ulster line, they were answered by the Irish Board of Works, that though this looked a little awkward, yet, in fact, the two ends being completed, there was little chance of the intervening part ever being finished, and that therefore there was no harm done. The dispute having been referred to General Pasley, he consulted all the leading authorities, and finally adopted five feet three inches as the national gauge for Ireland, being the mean of all their opinions, which differs from all the three gauges now in operation there.

FREDERICK S. WILLIAMS

77. CASEY JONES

Come *all* you rounders, if you wanta—*hear*
*Sto*ry a*bou*t a brave—*ing*ineer.

Now, "K. C."[1]—*Jones*—was this rounder's—*name*,
On a six-eight-wheeler, boys, he won—his—*fame*.
Caller called K.C. at a half-past—*four*,
Kissed his wife—at the station—*door*,
Mounted to the cabin with his orders in his hand,
Took his fare—well—trip—to the Promised—Land.

> *Casey—Jones!—Mounted to the cabin—*
> *Casey—Jones!—with his orders in his hand—*
> *Casey—Jones!—Mounted to the cabin—*
> *Took his farewell—trip, to the Promised—Land.*

"Put *in* yo' water, an' a-shovel in yo' *coal*,
Stick yo' head *out* the winda, watch them drivers—*roll*,
I'll *run* her—*till* she *leaves* the rail,
'Cause I'm eight hours *late* with that western—mail."
Looked *at* his *watch*, an' his watch was—*slow*;
Looked *at* the water, an' the *water* was low.
Turned to the fireman, an' then he—*said*,
'*We*'re gonna reach—Frisco, but we'll all—be—dead."

> *Casey—Jones!—Gonna reach—Frisco—*
> *Casey—Jones!—but we'll all—be dead—*
> *Casey—Jones!—Gonna reach—Frisco—*
> *Gonna reach—Frisco, but we'll all—be—dead.*

K.C. pulled *up*—that Reno—*hill*,
Whistled for the crossin' with an *aw*—ful shrill—
Switchman *knew*—by the ingine's *moans*—
That the man *at* the throttle *was* K. C. *Jones*.
Pulled up—within—two *miles* of the place—
Number *Four*—starin' him—right in the face!
Turned to the fireman, says, "Boy, better *jump*,
'Cause the's *two* locomotives that's a-gointa—*bump*!"

[1] K.C., Kansas City.

Casey—Jones!—Two—locomotives—
Casey—Jones!—that's a-gointa bump—
Casey—Jones!—Two—locomotives—
Two—Locomotives that's a-gointa—bump.

K.C. *said*—jes' befo' he—*died*,
"*Two—mo'*—roads, that I wanted to ride."
Fireman—says—"What *can* they—be?"
"It's the Southern—Pacific, an' the Santa—*Fe*."
Missis *Jones* sat *on*—her *bed*, a-sighin',
Jes' received a message that K.C. was dyin',
Says, "*Go* ta bed, chillun, an' *hush* yo' cryin',
'Cause you got another poppa on the Salt—Lake—Line."

Missis Casey—Jones!—Got another poppa—
Missis Casey—Jones!—on the Salt—Lake—Line—
Missis Casey—Jones!—Got another poppa—
Got another poppa on the Salt—Lake—Line.

AMERICAN FOLK-SONG

78. ASHTABULA—1876

A BLINDING north-easterly snow-storm, accompanied by a heavy wind, prevailed throughout the day which preceded the accident, greatly impeding the movement of trains. The Pacific express over the Michigan Southern & Lake Shore road had left Erie, going west, considerably behind its time, and had been started only with great difficulty and with the assistance of four locomotives. It was due at Ashtabula at about 5.30 o'clock P.M., but was three hours late, and, the days being then at their shortest, when it arrived at the bridge which was the scene of the accident the darkness was so great that nothing could be seen through the driving snow by those on the leading locomotive even for a distance of 50 feet ahead. The train was made up of two heavy locomotives, four baggage, mail and express cars, one smoking car, two ordinary coaches, a drawing-room car and three sleepers, being in all two locomotives and eleven cars, in the order named, containing, as nearly as can be ascertained, 190 human beings, of whom 170 were passengers. Ashtabula bridge is situated only about 1,000 feet east of the station of the same name, and spans a deep ravine, at the bottom of which flows a shallow stream, some two or three feet in depth, which empties into Lake Erie a mile or two away. The bridge was an iron Howe truss of 150 feet span, elevated 69 feet above the bottom of the ravine, and supported at either end by solid masonwork abutments. It had been built some fourteen years. As the train approached the bridge it had to force its way through a heavy snow-drift, and, when it passed on to it, it was moving at a speed of some twelve or fourteen miles an hour. The entire length of the bridge afforded space only for two of the express cars at most in addition to the locomotives, so that when the wheels of the leading locomotive rested on the western abutment of the bridge nine of the eleven cars which made up the train, including all those in which there were passengers, had yet to reach its eastern end. At the instant when the train stood in this position, the engineer of the leading locomotive heard a sudden cracking sound apparently beneath him, and thought he felt the bridge giving way. Instantly pulling the throttle valve wide open, his locomotive gave a spring forward and, as it did so, the bridge fell, the rear wheels of his tender falling with it. The jerk and impetus of the locomotive, however, sufficed to tear out the coupling, and as his tender was dragged up out of the abyss on to the track, though its rear wheels did not get upon the rails, the frightened engineer caught a fearful glimpse of the second locomotive as it seemed to turn and then fall bottom upwards into the ravine. The bridge had given way, not at once but by a slow sinking motion, which began at the point where the pressure was heaviest, under the two locomotives and at the west abutment. There being two tracks, and this train being on the southernmost of the two, the southern truss had first yielded, letting that side of the bridge down, and rolling, as it were, the second locomotive and the cars immediately behind it off to the left and quite clear of a straight line drawn between the two abutments; then almost immediately the other truss gave way and the whole bridge fell, but in doing so swung slightly to the right. Before this took place the entire train with the exception of the last two sleepers had reached the chasm, each car as it passed over falling nearer than the one which had preceded it to the east abutment, and finally the last two sleepers came, and, without being deflected from their course at all, plunged straight down and fell upon the wreck of the bridge at its east end. It was necessarily all the work of a few seconds.

At the bottom of the ravine the snow lay waist deep and the stream was covered with ice some eight inches in thickness. Upon this were piled up the fallen cars and engine, the latter on top of the former near the western abutment and upside down. All the passenger cars were heated by stoves. At first a dead silence seemed to follow the successive shocks of the falling mass. In less than two minutes, however, the fire began to show itself and within fifteen the holocaust was at its height. As usual, it was a mass of human beings, all more or less stunned, a few killed, many injured and helpless, and more yet simply pinned down to watch, in the possession as full as helpless of all their faculties, the rapid approach of the flames. The number of those killed outright seems to have been surprisingly small. In the last car, for instance, no one was lost. This was due to the energy and presence of mind of the porter, a negro named Steward, who, when he felt the car resting firmly on its side, broke a window and crawled through it, and then passed along breaking the other windows and extricating the passengers until all were gotten out. Those in the other cars were far less fortunate. Though an immediate alarm had been given in the neighboring town, the storm was so violent and the snow so deep that assistance arrived but slowly. Nor when it did arrive could much be effected. The essential thing was to extinguish the flames. The means for so doing were close at hand in a steam pump belonging to the railroad company, while an abundance of hose could have been procured at another place but a short distance off. In the excitement and agitation of the moment contradictory orders were given, even to forbidding the use of the pump, and practically no effort to extinguish the fire was made. Within half an hour of the accident the flames were at their height, and when the next morning dawned nothing remained in the ravine but a charred and undistinguishable mass of car trucks, brake-rods, twisted rails and bent and tangled bridge iron, with the upturned locomotive close to the west abutment.

C. F. ADAMS

79. THE WRECK OF THE OLD SOUTHERN 97

They give him—his *or*—ders at *Mon*roe, Virginia,
    Sayin' "*Pete*, you're *way* behin' *time*—
It is *not* Thirty-*Eight*, but it's ole Ninety-Seven,
    An' you put her in—center—*on time*."

He looked roun'—*said*, to his black, greasy fireman,
    Sayin' "Shove on in a little more—*coal*,
An *when* we *cross*—that White Oak—mountain,
    You kin watch ole Ninety-Seven—*roll*."

It's a mighty rough *road*—from Lynchburg—to Danville,
　　An' a-lyin' on a three—mile—*grade*.
It was on that—grade—that he lost his air-brakes,
　　An' you see what—a *jump*—he—*made*.

She was goin' down—grade—makin' *ninety* miles an hour,
　　When her whistle broke—*into*—a *scream*—
He was found—in the wreck, with his hand on the throttle,
　　An' a-scalded to *death*—with the steam.

Now, *la*—*dies*—you *must* take warning,
　　From this time now, an' *learn*—
Never *speak*—harsh—*words* to your kin' lovin' husban',
　　He may leave you, an' *never*—return.

AMERICAN FOLK-SONG

80. A MASSACRE OF INNOCENTS

But suddenly there was an interruption. Presley had climbed the fence at the limit of the Quien Sabe ranch. Beyond was Los Muertos, but between the two ran the railroad. He had only time to jump back upon the embankment when, with a quivering of all the earth, a locomotive, single, unattached, shot by him with a roar, filling the air with the reek of hot oil, vomiting smoke and sparks; its enormous eye, cyclopean, red, throwing a glare far in advance, shooting by in a sudden crash of confused thunder; filling the night with the terrific clamour of its iron hoofs.

Abruptly Presley remembered. This must be the crack passenger engine of which Dyke had told him, the one delayed by the accident on the Bakersfield division, for whose passage the track had been opened all the way to Fresno.

Before Presley could recover from the shock of the irruption, while the earth was still vibrating, the rails still humming, the engine was far away, flinging the echo of its frantic gallop over all the valley. For a brief instant it roared with a hollow diapason on the Long Trestle over Broderson Creek, then plunged into a cutting farther on, the quivering glare of its fires losing itself in the night, its thunder abruptly diminishing to a subdued and distant humming. All at once this ceased. The engine was gone.

But the moment the noise of the engine lapsed, Presley—about to start forward again—was conscious of a confusion of lamentable sounds that rose into the night from out the engine's wake. Prolonged cries of agony, sobbing wails of infinite pain, heart-rending, pitiful.

The noises came from a little distance. He ran down the track, crossing the culvert, over the irrigating ditch, and at the head of the long reach of track—between the culvert and the Long Trestle—paused abruptly, held immovable at the sight of the ground and rails all about him.

In some way, the herd of sheep—Vanamee's herd—had found a breach in the wire fence by the right of way and had wandered out upon the tracks. A band had been crossing just at the moment of the engine's passage. The pathos of it was beyond expression. It was a slaughter, a massacre of innocents. The iron monster had charged full into the midst, merciless, inexorable. To the right and left, all the width of the right of way, the little bodies had been flung; backs were snapped against the fence posts; brains knocked out. Caught in the barbs of the wire, wedged in, the bodies hung suspended. Under foot it was terrible. The black blood, winking in the starlight, seeped down into the clinkers between the ties with a prolonged sucking murmur.

Presley turned away, horror-struck, sick at heart, overwhelmed with a quick burst of irresistible compassion for this brute agony he could not relieve. The sweetness was gone from the evening, the sense of peace, of security, and placid contentment was stricken from the landscape. The hideous ruin in the engine's path drove all thought of his poem from his mind. The inspiration vanished like a mist. The *de Profundis* had ceased to ring.

He hurried across the Los Muertos ranch, almost running, even putting his hands over his ears till he was out of hearing distance of that all but human distress. Not until he was beyond ear-shot did he pause, looking back, listening. The night had shut down again. For a moment the silence was profound, unbroken.

Then, faint and prolonged, across the levels of the ranch, he heard the engine whistling for Bonneville. Again and again, at rapid intervals in its flying course, it whistled for road crossings, for sharp curves, for trestles; ominous notes, hoarse, bellowing, ringing with the accents of menace and defiance; and abruptly Presley saw again, in his imagination, the galloping monster, the terror of steel and steam, with its single eye, cyclopean, red, shooting from horizon to horizon; but saw it now as the symbol of a vast power, huge, terrible, flinging the echo of its thunder over all the reaches of the valley, leaving blood and destruction in its path; the leviathan, with tentacles of steel clutching into the soil, the soulless Force, the iron-hearted Power, the monster, the Colossus, the Octopus.

FRANK NORRIS

81. DAID AN' GONE

On a Monday mawnin' it begunta—*rain*,
Roun'—the *bend*—come a passenger train—
On—the bumpers *was* a hobo—*Jawn*,
He was a good ole—*hobo*, but he's daid an'—*gone*.

Daid an'—gone—
Daid an'—gone—
He was a good ole—hobo, but he's daid an'—gone.

Old Bill Jones *was* a good ing*ineer*,
Says to his fireman, "Jim, yo' needn'ta fear,
All Ah want, is my boilers—*hot*,
Gunna mek it to the junction *bah*—twelve o'—clock.

Twelve—o'—clock—
Twelve—o'—clock—
Gunna mek it to the junction bah—twelve o'—clock."

Jay Gould's daughter—*said*, jes' befo' she *died*,
"Poppa, *fix* the blinds so's the *bums* cain't ride!
Ef ride—they *mus'*, let 'm ride the—*rods*,
Let 'm put their—*trus'*—in the hands of—*God.*"

Hands—of God—
Hands—of God—
Let 'm put their—trus'—in the hands of—God.

AMERICAN FOLK-SONG

82. COLLISION AT THORPE

A TERMINUS collision took place at Thorpe, between Norwich
and Great Yarmouth, on the Great Eastern Railway in England, on the 10th of September, 1874. The line had in this
place but a single track, and the mail train from Norwich, under
the rule, had to wait at a station called Brundell until the
arrival there of the evening express from Yarmouth, or until
it received permission by the telegraph to proceed. On the
evening of the disaster the express train was somewhat behind
its time, and the inspector wrote a dispatch directing the mail

to come forward without waiting for it. This dispatch he left in the telegraph office unsigned, while he went to attend to other matters. Just then the express train came along, and he at once allowed it to proceed. Hardly was it under way when the unsigned dispatch occurred to him, and the unfortunate man dashed to the telegraph office only to learn that the operator had forwarded it. Under the rules of the company no return message was required. A second dispatch was instantly sent to Brundell to stop the mail; the reply came back that the mail was gone. A collision was inevitable.

The two trains were of very equal weight, the one consisting of fourteen and the other of thirteen carriages. They were both drawn by powerful locomotives, the drivers of which had reason for putting on an increased speed, believing, as each had cause to believe, that the other was waiting for him. The night was intensely dark and it was raining heavily, so that, even if the brakes were applied, the wheels would slide along the slippery track. Under these circumstances the two trains rushed upon each other around a slight curve which sufficed to conceal their head-lights. The combined momentum must have amounted to little less than sixty miles an hour, and the shock was heard through all the neighboring villages. The smoke-stack of the locomotive drawing the mail train was swept away as the other locomotive seemed to rush on top of it, while the carriages of both trains followed until a mound of locomotives and shattered cars was formed which the descending torrents alone hindered from becoming a funeral pyre. So sudden was the collision that the driver of one of the engines did not apparently have an opportunity to shut off the steam, and his locomotive, though forced from the track and disabled, yet remained some time in operation in the midst of the wreck. In both trains, very fortunately, there were a number of empty cars between the locomotives and the carriages in which the passengers were seated, and they were utterly demolished; but for this fortunate circumstance the Thorpe collision might well have proved the most disastrous of all railroad accidents. As it was, the men on both the locomotives were instantly killed, together with seventeen passengers, and four other passengers subsequently died of their injuries; making a total of twenty-five deaths, besides fifty cases of injury.

It would be difficult to conceive of a more violent collision than that which has just been described; and yet, as curiously illustrating the rapidity with which the force of the most severe shock is expended, it is said that two gentlemen in the last carriage of one of the trains, finding it at a sudden standstill close to the place to which they were going, supposed it had stopped for some unimportant cause and concluded to take advantage of a happy chance which left them almost at the doors of their homes. They accordingly got out and hurried away in the rain, learning only the next morning of the catastrophe in which they had been unconscious participants.

C. F. ADAMS

83. THE FREIGHT WRECK AT ALTOONA, PA.

She had just—left the point at Kit*tan*ning—
    The freight—Number Twelve—Sixty-*Two*—
An' *on* the mountain—she travelled,
    An' brave—were the *men*—in her crew.

The en—gineer *pulled*—at the whistle,
    For the brakes—wouldn't work—when applied—
An' the brake—man climbed out—on those car-tops,
    For he *knew*—what that *whistle*—had cried.

With *all*—of the strength—that God gave him,
   He tight—ened the brakes—with a prayer—
But the train—kep' right on—down the mountain,
   An' her whist—le was *pier*—cin' the air.

She trav—elled at *six*—ty an hower—
   Gainin' speed—every foot *of* the way,
An' then—with a *crash*—it was over—
   An' there—on the track—the freight lay.

Now it's not—the amount—of the damage,
   Nor the val—ue of what—it all *cost,*
It's the *sad* tale that came—from the cabin,
   Where the lives—of two *brave* men were lost.

They were found—at their posts, in the wreckage—
   They died—when the en—gine had fell:
The en—gineer *still*—held the whistle—
   An' the fireman—still *hung* to the bell.

This sto—ry is told—of a freight-train,
   An' *should*—be a *war*—ning to all—
You must—be prepared—every momint,
   For *you*—cannot tell—when He'll *call.*

AMERICAN FOLK-SONG

84. THE TAY BRIDGE DISASTER, 1879

Beautiful Railway Bridge of the Silv'ry Tay!
Alas! I am very sorry to say
That ninety lives have been taken away,
On the last Sabbath day of 1879
Which will be remember'd for a very long time.

When the train left Edinburgh
The passengers' hearts were light and felt no sorrow,
But Boreas blew a terrific gale,
Which made their hearts for to quail,
And many of the passengers with fear did say—
"I hope God will send us safe across the Bridge of Tay."

So the train mov'd slowly along the Bridge of Tay,
Until it was about midway,
Then the central girders with a crash gave way,
And down went the train and passengers into the Tay!
The Storm Fiend did loudly bray,
Because ninety lives had been taken away,
On the last Sabbath day of 1879,
Which will be remember'd for a very long time.

It must have been an awful sight,
To witness in the dusky moonlight,
While the Storm Fiend did laugh, and angry did bray,
Along the Railway Bridge of the Silv'ry Tay.
I must now conclude my lay
By telling the world fearlessly without the least dismay,
That your central girders would not have given away,
At least many sensible men do say,
Had they been supported on each side with buttresses,
At least many sensible men confesses,
For the stronger we our houses do build,
The less chance we have of being killed.

WILLIAM MCGONAGALL
Poet and Tragedian

85. AFTERMATH

BY private letter from Utsue, an island on the western coast
of Norway, is communicated to Dapposten the intelligence

that on the 12th inst. some fishermen pulled on the Firth to haul their nets, and had hardly finished their labour when they sighted an extraordinary object some distance further out. The superstitious fears of sea monsters which have been written a good deal about lately held them back for some time, but their curiosity made them approach the supposed sea monster, and, to their great surprise, they found that it was something like a building. As the sea was calm they immediately commenced to tow it to shore, where it was hauled up on the beach and was then found to be a damaged railway wagon. The wheels were off, the windows smashed, and one door hanging on its hinges. By the name on it, "Edinburgh and Glasgow Railway," it was at once surmised that it must have been one of the wagons separated from the train which met with the disaster on the Tay Bridge. In the carriage was a portmanteau containing garments, some of them marked "P.B." The wagon was sent, on the 14th, to Hangesund, to be forwarded thence to Bergen.

MORGENBLEDET, 20th February 1880

86. MALINES. MIDNIGHT

4th July, 1882

Belgian, with cumbrous tread and iron boots,
Who in the murky middle of the night,
Designing to renew the foul pursuits
In which thy life is passed, ill-favoured wight,
And wishing on the platform to alight
Where thou couldst mingle with thy fellow brutes,
Didst walk the carriage floor (a leprous sight),
As o'er the sky some baleful meteor shoots:
Upon my slippered foot thou didst descend,
Didst rouse me from my slumbers mad with pain,

And laughedst loud for several minutes' space.
Oh may'st thou suffer tortures without end:
May fiends with glowing pincers rend thy brain,
And beetles batten on thy blackened face!

J. K. STEPHEN

87. ROYALTY TO THE RESCUE

A DISPATCH from Sofia tonight says that the King of Bulgaria had an exciting adventure today. He was travelling to Varna, and the train, in which he was an ordinary passenger, had just reached Strazica Station when he heard a report that the driver was in imminent danger of losing his life, as the engine had caught fire, and he was lying injured with his clothes blazing, and that no one dared approach. The King instantly rushed to the engine, rescued the man, and tore the clothes from his body. The man was badly burned, but his life is believed to have been saved by the King's presence of mind and daring.

King Boris, who is an expert driver, later mounted the engine and himself drove the train to Varna.

THE TIMES, Wednesday, 31 October 1934

88. A DRIVER'S SKILL

IT was a hot summer's morning in the early days of the war when, at about nine o'clock, I joined at Crewe the Liverpool train to Euston. We had *Princess Royal* to take us. Just after Stafford I went to the dining-car, the third coach from the front, for coffee. We were about to drink it when suddenly the dining-car seemed to bounce. The coffee spilled all over the tables and everybody jumped to their feet. Mindful of the grisly stories I had heard of seats buckling in accidents and trapping one's legs, I got quickly into the gang-way and told the man next to me to do the same. The brakes went on, not very hard, but they stayed on, and the speed gradually fell. Still, we seemed to be running all right. We ran under a bridge, but were steadily losing way, and we stopped about two miles south of Atherstone exactly oppo-site the long red brick wall of what turned out to be a laundry. Except for that alarming bounce, it had felt simply as though we had been brought to a standstill by a signal, in fact for a few moments that was exactly what I thought had happened, and a look through the top sliding panels of the window (for you cannot let down the window of a dining-car) revealed nothing out of the ordinary.

A further look showed unmistakably that something was seriously wrong. The driver, a short, grey-haired man, jumped down from his engine, and ran back a few yards to a point where he could see the full length of his train. He took one look at it, and ran back to his engine, calling to his fire-man as he ran; and he, in turn, jumped off the footplate and bolted to the nearest signal box. The dining-car steward came along calling "Are there any doctors on the train?" and so no doubt was left that this was more than a signal check. At that point I got out on to the line to see for myself. Our dining-car was still on the rails, but nothing behind us was. The next coach had one bogie off, and after that the line simply did not exist any more. Steel rails were bent into fantastic shapes, sleepers were uprooted, the ballast was scored and ploughed by the wheels of a dozen coaches which for several hundred yards had been hauled straight through it. The rails of two of the other three tracks had also been forced out of position, and the rear coaches were slewed across the two down tracks. Only the slow up-line was still clear. The back two coaches, swaying violently as they ran on the ballast, had struck the bridge glancing blows. Their springs were smashed and their windows splintered. Incredibly, there were only two minor casualties in all that long and crowded train. Two women in the last coach had been cut by flying glass, and apart from one or two cases of shock, that was all. That driver had hauled his fifteen coaches for nearly half a mile from a speed of seventy miles an hour to a dead stop on a track which was simply sleepers and ballast and jagged rail ends, and under a bridge, which the rear coaches had struck, and he had contrived to halt the train with every coach upright and every coupling intact. It was a marvellous feat, and to his skill alone several hundred people owe their limbs and their lives.

CANON ROGER LLOYD

Trains of Thought

89. STEAM'S TRIUMPHAL CAR

Lay down your rails, ye nations, near and far—
Yoke your full trains to Steam's triumphal car;
Link town to town; unite in iron bands
The long-estranged and oft-embattled lands.
Peace, mild-eyed seraph—Knowledge, light divine,
Shall send their messengers by every line.
Men, join'd in amity, shall wonder long
That Hate had power to lead their fathers wrong;
Or that false Glory lured their hearts astray,
And made it virtuous and sublime to slay. . .
Blessings on Science, and her handmaid Steam!
They make Utopia only half a dream.

CHARLES MACKAY

90. FOR WHAT GOOD END?

Gryllus:
I see long trains of strange machines on wheels,
With one in front of each, puffing white smoke

125

From a black, hollow column. Fast and far
They speed, like yellow leaves before the gale,
When autumn winds are strongest. Through their windows
I judge them thronged with people; but distinctly
Their speed forbids my seeing.
Spirit-Rapper: This is one
Of the great glories of our modern time.
"Men are become as birds," and skim like swallows
The surface of the world.
Gryllus: For what good end?
Spirit-Rapper:
The end is in itself—the end of skimming
The surface of the world.

THOMAS LOVE PEACOCK

91. THE MODERN HOTSPUR

The modern Hotspur
Shrills not his trumpet of "To Horse, To Horse!"
But consults columns in a Railway Guide;
A demigod of figures; an Achilles
Of computation;
A verier Mercury, express come down
To do the world with swift arithmetic.

ARTHUR HUGH CLOUGH

92. LIFE IS VERY LIKE A RAILWAY

ARE you aware that life is very like a railway? One gets into
deep cuttings and long dark tunnels, where one sees nothing
and hears twice as much noise as usual, and one can't read,
and one shuts up the window, and waits, and then it all comes
clear again. Only in life it sometimes feels as if one had to
dig the tunnel as one goes along, all new for oneself. Go

straight on, however, and one's sure to come out into a new country, on the other side the hills, sunny and bright. There's an apologue for you!

ARTHUR HUGH CLOUGH

93. ORDERED SOUTH

By a curious irony of fate, the places to which we are sent when health deserts us are often singularly beautiful. Often, too, they are places we have visited in former years, or seen briefly in passing by, and kept ever afterwards in pious memory; and we please ourselves with the fancy that we shall repeat many vivid and pleasurable sensations, and take up again the thread of our enjoyment in the same spirit as we let it fall. We shall now have an opportunity of finishing many pleasant excursions, interrupted of yore before our curiosity was fully satisfied. It may be that we have kept in mind, during all these years, the recollection of some valley into which we have just looked down for a moment before we lost sight of it in the disorder of the hills; it may be that we have lain awake at night, and agreeably tantalised ourselves with the thought of corners we had never turned, or summits we had all but climbed: we shall now be able, as we tell ourselves, to complete all these unfinished pleasures, and pass beyond the barriers that confined our recollections.

The promise is so great, and we are all so easily led away when hope and memory are both in one story, that I dare say the sick man is not very inconsolable when he receives sentence of banishment, and is inclined to regard his ill-health as not the least fortunate accident of his life. Nor is he immediately undeceived. The stir and speed of the journey, and the restlessness that goes to bed with him as he tries to sleep between two days of noisy progress, fever him, and stimulate his dull nerves into something of their old quickness and sensibility. And so he can enjoy the faint autumnal splendour of the landscape, as he sees hill and plain, vineyard and forest, clad in one wonderful glory of fairy gold, which the first great winds of winter will transmute, as in the fable, into withered leaves. And so too he can enjoy the admirable brevity and simplicity of such little glimpses of country and country ways as flash upon him through the windows of the train; little glimpses that have a character all their own; sights seen as a travelling swallow might see them from the wing, or Iris as she went abroad over the land on some Olympian errand. Here and there, indeed, a few children huzzah and wave their hands to the express; but for the most part it is an interruption too brief and isolated to attract much notice; the sheep do not cease from browsing; a girl sits balanced on the projecting tiller of a canal boat, so precariously that it seems as if a fly or the splash of a leaping fish would be enough to overthrow the dainty equilibrium, and yet all these hundreds of tons of coal and wood and iron have been precipitated roaring past her very ear, and there is not a start, not a tremor, not a turn of the averted head, to indicate that she has been even conscious of its passage.

Herein, I think, lies the chief attraction of railway travel. The speed is so easy, and the train disturbs so little the scenes through which it takes us, that our heart becomes full of the placidity and stillness of the country; and while the body is borne forward in the flying chain of carriages, the thoughts alight, as the humour moves them, at unfrequented stations; they make haste up the poplar alley that leads towards the town; they are left behind with the signalman as, shading his eyes with his hand, he watches the long train sweep away into the golden distance.

ROBERT LOUIS STEVENSON

94. A LOCAL TRAIN OF THOUGHT

Alone, in silence, at a certain time of night,
Listening, and looking up from what I'm trying to write,
I hear a local train along the Valley. And "There
Goes the one-fifty," think I to myself; aware
That somehow its habitual travelling comforts me,
Making my world seem safer, homelier, sure to be
The same to-morrow; and the same, one hopes, next year.
"There's peacetime in that train." One hears it disappear
With needless warning whistle and rail-resounding wheels.
"That train's quite like an old familiar friend," one feels.

SIEGFRIED SASSOON

95. EXPRESS

As the through-train of words with white-hot whistle
Shrills past the heart's mean halts, the mind's full stops,
With all the signals down; past the small town
Contentment, and the citizens all leaning
And loitering parenthetically
In waiting-rooms, or interrogative on platforms;
Its screaming mouth crammed tight with urgent meaning,
—I, by it borne on, look out and wonder
To what happy or calamitous terminus
I am bound, what anonymity or what renown.

O if at length into Age, the last of all stations,
It slides and slows, and its smoky mane of thunder
Thins out, and I detrain; when I stand in that place
On whose piers and wharves, from all sources and seas,
Men wearily arrive—I pray that still
I may have with me my pities and indignations.

W. R. RODGERS

Trains of Triumph, Trains of Fate

96. NON-STOP TO PETERLOO

SEPTEMBER 1ST, 1842. . . . Parliament was no sooner up, than the riots broke out, sufficiently alarming but for the railroads, which enabled the Government to pour troops into the disturbed districts, and extinguish the conflagration at once. . . .

CHARLES GREVILLE

ON Saturday, August 13th, there was fierce rioting in Rochdale, Tolmorden, Bury, Macclesfield, Bolton, Stockport, Burslem and Hanley. At the latter place 5000 strikers marched on a neighbouring country mansion and left it blazing. Hordes of rough-looking men in fur caps carrying clubs and faggots patrolled the squalid unpaved roads around the idle mills; others attempted to hold up the mail and tear up the permanent way on the Manchester–Leeds railway. Next morning, though Sunday, the Cabinet met and issued urgent orders to the Guards and the Artillery at Woolwich to hold themselves in readiness for Manchester. That evening as the 3rd battalion of the Grenadiers debouched with band playing through the gates of St. George's Barracks into Trafalgar Square, vast numbers of working men and boys closed in and tried to obstruct its progress. In Regent Street the crowd became so menacing that the order was given to fix bayonets; all the way to Euston Square Station, which was packed with police, hisses and groans continued. The 34th Foot, summoned in haste from Portsmouth, was also continuously hooted on its march across London.

By the evening of the 16th, Manchester was held by three regular infantry battalions, the 1st Royal Dragoons and artillery detachments with howitzers and six-pounders. A few miles away the streets of Bolton were patrolled by companies of the 72nd Highlanders. Other troops poured in by the new railroads with such rapidity that the rebellion quickly began to lose its dangerous appearance. All that week the magistrates and police, protected by the military, were busy arresting ringleaders and detachments of rioters, and every main road and railway was watched by mounted constables and dragoons.

After that the insurrection crumbled. Further resort to force was useless. Hunger did the rest. . . .

ARTHUR BRYANT

97. CHARLES PEACE ESCAPES

THE murderer and burglar, who was one of the most startling products of modern society, was taken, on January 22, 1879 —after his capture by Sergeant Robinson on the lawn in St. John's Park, Blackheath—by train on his way to Sheffield, where he was to undergo examination before the magistrates for the murder of Arthur Dyson, civil engineer, at Banner Cross.

The notoriety of the criminal had become almost the country's talk. His resource and daring were on everybody's tongue. "It would be a funny thing if he escaped," said a spectator, chatting to an official in the Sheffield Police Court, which was crammed with a crowd waiting in eager expectation for the prisoner's arrival. Scarcely were the words uttered than there was an indescribable flutter in the Court, much whispering, and many serious faces. Charles Peace had escaped! All the way down from Pentonville the man, who was restless, savage, and snarling, just like a wild beast, gave the warders continual trouble. When the Great Northern express was speeding through the pastoral country a little north of Worksop, Peace, jibing and sneering at his gaolers, sprang to the carriage window and took a flying leap out of the express. But his panther-like action availed him little. The under-warder seized him by the left foot as he leapt from the compartment, and held on with desperate grasp. The other warder tugged at the communication-cord, but it would not act.

On went the express by field and homestead, the driver unaware of the fierce struggle behind. Peace, suspended head downward, with his face banging now and then against the oscillating carriage, tried with his right leg to kick himself free from the warder's grip. The struggling attracted the attention of the passengers, but they could do nothing to assist the warder, who, with every muscle quivering, was straining with his writhing prisoner. Shout after shout passed from carriage to carriage, only to be carried miles away by the wind; the noise of the clamouring travellers simply made strange echoes in the driver's ears. For two miles the struggle went on; then Peace, determined to end it, whatever the result to himself, wriggled his left foot out of his shoe, which was left in the warder's grasp, and at last he was free. He fell wildly, his head struck the carriage footboard with tremendous force, and he bounded into the six-foot, where he rolled over and over, a curious bundle half enveloped in a cloud of dust.

Still onward sped the train, the warder, helpless to secure his prey, craning his neck as far as he could out of the carriage window, his face a study of rage and concern because he had been outwitted. Nearly another mile was covered before the express pulled up. No time was then lost in chasing the fugitive. The warders, accompanied by several passengers eager for adventure, ran back along the line and found Peace in the six-foot, not far from the place at which he had made his reckless descent from the train. The man was lying near the down track, a huddled heap, unconscious, with a serious wound in his head. He was not merely a person of amazing unscrupulousness, but of wondrous vitality, and he soon recovered sensibility, murmuring, as he was lifted into the guard's van of a goods train for removal to Sheffield, "I am cold; cover me up." The warders were only too pleased to cover him up; they took every care of him. When he was conveyed to Armley in readiness for his trial they were armed with revolvers; but the "small, elderly-looking, feeble man, in brown convict-dress," made no further attempt to escape. He was sentenced to death at Leeds assizes and hanged, no one regretting the hardened criminal's doom.

JOHN PENDLETON

98. TO THE FINLAND STATION

HEAVILY guarded, a sealed car races from the Swiss border through Germany with a deadly cargo for Russia. Today every child would recognize the strange bald Slavic head with the enormous cranium that cradled a World Revolution. In

April, 1917, maddest and most fateful month of the war, Vladimir Ulianov, called Lenin, was unknown, except to the secret police and to the small group of radicals, socialists, syndicalists and nihilists who made the overthrow of the Czar their vocation. At the request of Bethmann Hollweg, Ludendorff granted Lenin and his twenty-eight garrulous followers safe transit through Germany to increase the embarrassments of Russia. . . .

No one took the émigrés, jabbering in many tongues, seriously. Nevertheless, the fate of three Empires, maybe the fate of the world—certainly the current of thought for centuries to come—was determined by twenty-nine intellectual vagabonds travelling to Russia by the grace of Ludendorff with a German safe-conduct.

The curtains of the sealed car that carried Lenin and his retinue were tightly drawn, the corridors occupied by German soldiers. In the dimly lighted compartments the Bolsheviks debated the impending doom of the bourgeoisie as they had done for decades. The German officer in charge of the coach gazed in astonishment at the unkempt bearded foreigners, who were whisked without passports mysteriously through the land.

Leaning against his cushioned seat, Lenin's eyes vainly attempted to pierce the curtain. What fate awaited him in Russia? Would he be cheered as a saviour or shot as a traitor? . . .

According to regulations, strictly enforced by the German crew, smoking in the coach was forbidden. Several Bolshevist ideologists who could not think without belching like chimneys monopolized the toilet of the car for the enjoyment of secret smokes to the annoyance of certain "comrades" who had other, legitimate uses for this convenience.

Suddenly the world-encircling reveries of the High Priest of Marx were punctuated by loud curses and high-pitched disputations. That in itself was not surprising. The Bolshevists were always gabbing and gabbling over fine theoretical points, like medieval theologians who could not agree on the precise number of angels capable of dancing on the point of a needle.

A crisis was plainly at hand. Two committees representing the two hostile groups, presented the dispute to their exalted leader. The Menshevik leader Abramovitch, who had managed to join the Bolsheviki, cited Marx; Zinoviev retorted with quotations from Engels. Russia's future Dictator, equal to the occasion, tore a sheet of paper into small scraps. These scraps, signed by him, were passes to the toilet. He issued only one pass for smoking to every three passes for the other purely natural physiological needs. That revealed his sturdy common-sense. His decision restored the tranquillity of the comrades. After Lenin's death they resumed their bickerings. They did not stop quarrelling until Stalin stopped their mouths for ever.

GEORGE SYLVESTER VIERECK

99. BLOWING UP TRAINS

In the best circumstances, waiting for action was hard. To-day it was beastly. Even enemy patrols stumbled along without care, perfunctorily against the rain. At last, near noon, in a snatch of fine weather, the watchmen on the south peak flagged their cloaks wildly in signal of a train. We reached our positions in an instant, for we had squatted the late hours on our heels in a streaming ditch near the line, so as not to miss another chance. The Arabs took cover properly. I looked back at their ambush from my firing point, and saw nothing but the grey hill-sides.

I could not hear the train coming, but trusted, and knelt

ready for perhaps half an hour, when the suspense became intolerable, and I signalled to know what was up. They sent down to say it was coming very slowly, and was an enormously long train. Our appetites stiffened. The longer it was the more would be the loot. Then came word that it had stopped. It moved again.

Finally, near one o'clock, I heard it panting. The locomotive was evidently defective (all these wood-fired trains were bad), and the heavy load on the up-gradient was proving too much for its capacity. I crouched behind my bush, while it crawled slowly into view past the south cutting, and along the bank above my head towards the culvert. The first ten trucks were open trucks, crowded with troops. However, once again it was too late to choose, so when the engine was squarely over the mine I pushed down the handle of the exploder. Nothing happened. I sawed it up and down four times.

Still nothing happened; and I realized that it had gone out of order, and that I was kneeling on a naked bank, with a Turkish troop train crawling past fifty yards away. The bush, which had seemed a foot high, shrank smaller than a fig-leaf; and I felt myself the most distinct object in the country-side. Behind me was an open valley for two hundred yards to the cover where my Arabs were waiting and wondering what I was at. It was impossible to make a bolt for it, or the Turks would step off the train and finish us. If I sat still, there might be just a hope of my being ignored as a casual Bedouin.

So there I sat, counting for sheer life, while eighteen open trucks, three box-waggons, and three officers' coaches dragged by. The engine panted slower and slower, and I thought every moment that it would break down. The troops took no great notice of me, but the officers were interested, and came out to the little platforms at the ends of their carriages, pointing and staring. I waved back at them, grinning nervously, and feeling an improbable shepherd in my Meccan dress, with its twisted golden circlet about my head. Perhaps the mud-stains, the wet and their ignorance made me accepted. The end of the brake van slowly disappeared into the cutting on the north.

As it went, I jumped up, buried my wires, snatched hold of the wretched exploder, and went like a rabbit uphill into safety. There I took breath and looked back to see that the train had finally stuck. It waited, about five hundred yards beyond the mine, for nearly an hour to get up a head of steam, while an officers' patrol came back and searched, very carefully, the ground where I had been sitting. However the wires were properly hidden: they found nothing: the engine plucked up heart again, and away they went. . .

Just at that moment the watchman on the north cried a train. We left the fire and made a breathless race of the six hundred yards down hill to our old position. Round the bend, whistling its loudest, came the train, a splendid two-engined thing of twelve passenger coaches, travelling at top speed on the favouring grade. I touched off under the first driving wheel of the first locomotive, and the explosion was terrific. The ground spouted blackly into my face, and I was sent spinning, to sit up with the shirt torn to my shoulder and the blood dripping from long ragged scratches on my left arm. Between my knees lay the exploder, crushed under a twisted sheet of sooty iron. In front of me was the scalded and smoking upper half of a man. When I peered through the dust and steam of the explosion the whole boiler of the first engine seemed to be missing.

I dully felt that it was time to get away to support; but when I moved, learnt that there was a great pain in my right foot, because of which I could only limp along, with my head swinging from the shock. Movement began to clear away this confusion, as I hobbled towards the upper valley, whence the Arabs were now shooting fast into the crowded coaches. Dizzily I cheered myself by repeating aloud in English "Oh, I wish this hadn't happened."

When the enemy began to return our fire, I found myself much between the two. Ali saw me fall, and thinking that I was hard hit, ran out, with Turki and about twenty men of his servants and the Beni Sakhr, to help me. The Turks found their range and got seven of them in a few seconds. The others, in a rush, were about me—fit models, after their activity, for a sculptor. Their full white cotton drawers drawn in, bell-like, round their slender waists and ankles, their hairless brown bodies; and the love-locks plaited tightly over each temple in long horns, made them look like Russian dancers.

We scrambled back into cover together, and there, secretly, I felt myself over, to find I had not once been really hurt; though besides the bruises and cuts of the boiler-plate and a broken toe, I had five different bullet-grazes on me (some of them uncomfortably deep) and my clothes ripped to pieces.

From the watercourse we could look about. The explosion had destroyed the arched head of the culvert, and the frame of the first engine was lying beyond it, at the near foot of the embankment down which it had rolled. The second loco- motive had toppled into the gap, and was lying across the ruined tender of the first. Its bed was twisted. I judged them both beyond repair. The second tender had disappeared over the further side; and the first three waggons had telescoped and were smashed in pieces.

The rest of the train was badly derailed, with the listing coaches butted end to end at all angles, zigzagged along the track. One of them was a saloon, decorated with flags. In it had been Mehmed Jemal Pasha, commanding the Eighth Army Corps, hurrying down to defend Jerusalem against

Allenby. His chargers had been in the first waggon; his motor-car was on the end of the train, and we shot it up. Of his staff we noticed a fat ecclesiastic, whom we thought to be Assad Shukair, Imam to Ahmed Jemal Pasha, and a notorious pro-Turk pimp. So we blazed at him till he dropped.

T. E. LAWRENCE

100. MELODRAMA AT COMPIÈGNE

HITLER summoned the French representatives yesterday to hear his terms for France. In his hour of triumph Hitler has scorned no detail of revenge or drama. The French representatives were taken to the woods of Compiègne—to the drab railway carriage which, unchanged since the day when Marshal Foch handed the Allied terms of surrender to the defeated Germans, has stood at Rethondes as a simple memorial of the victory won by Allied valour and Allied unity.

Hitler took Foch's chair yesterday. He had arrived at the carriage at 2.45. A large area round the carriage had been railed off and guarded by sentries. Near the carriage was a large tent, with tables and chairs for the French delegates and a large notice reminding them of the date—June 21, 1940—as though to expunge the previous date of 1918. Near at hand the plaque commemorating the signature of the 1918 armistice had been covered by the war standard of the German Reich, and in front of it was flying Hitler's own standard. Two platoons of infantry and an Air Force contingent were drawn up outside the carriage. Field-Marshal Göring, head of the German Air Force, Grand Admiral Raeder, commanding the German Navy, General Von Brauchitsch, Commander-in-Chief of the Army, General Keitel, Chief of Staff of the

Supreme Command of the Army, Ribbentrop, the Foreign Minister, and Hess, Hitler's Deputy, were all in attendance.

After the military commander had given him a short address of welcome on behalf of "the great German armed forces" Hitler went into the carriage. Soon afterwards the French delegates—General Huntziger, General Bergeret, Admiral Leluc, and M. Noel—were taken in, and were greeted by Hitler with the raised arm salute. According to the German account General Huntziger hesitated for a moment before entering the car. In the presence of Hitler, General Keitel then stood up and read the Führer's introductory message, the preamble to the message, and the terms themselves. . . .

The German News Agency, commenting on the scene, asserted:

> Today's act in the forest of Compiègne has eradicated the injustice committed against the honour of German arms. The dignity of the procedure towards an honourably defeated opponent was in sharp contrast to the monument erected at this spot in which Gallic spite had insulted the German Army.

The tablet which was added to the saloon car by the French after 1918 bore the inscription: "Here on November 11, 1918, succumbed the criminal pride of the German Empire, vanquished by the free peoples it attempted to enslave."

THE TIMES, Saturday, 22 June 1940

101. AMMUNITION TRAIN

I FORGET which of us it was who found the ammunition train. There were two of them, as a matter of fact, lying forlornly in a railway siding outside the town of Larissa. Larissa in the great empty plain of Thessaly was our main supply base in northern Greece, from which, in April 1941, we were with-drawing under heavy German pressure.

The town had been bombed by the Italians, then it had been badly damaged by an earthquake, and now it was receiving regular attention from the Luftwaffe. It was an awful mess. The Greek railway staff had run away and it was pretty obvious that the two ammunition trains had been abandoned. I knew that we were seriously short of ammu-nition further down the line, so I went to the Brigadier in charge of the base and asked permission to try to get one of the trains away. It was given with alacrity.

I don't want you to think that this action on my part was public-spirited, or anything like that. My motives were purely selfish. We wanted a job. We were a small unit which had been carrying out various irregular activities further north; but now the sort of tasks for which we were designed had become impossible, and we were in danger of becoming what civil servants call redundant. We felt that if we could get this train away we should be doing something useful and justifying our existence. Besides, one of us claimed that he knew how to drive an engine.

This was Norman Johnstone, a brother officer in the Grenadier Guards. One of our jobs earlier in the campaign had been to destroy some rolling-stock which could not be moved away. Norman had a splendid time blowing up about twenty valuable locomotives and a lot of trucks, but towards the end we ran out of explosives. At this stage a sergeant in the 4th Hussars turned up, who was an engine-driver in civilian life. With Norman helping him, he got steam up in the four surviving engines, drove them a quarter of a mile down the line, then sent them full tilt back into the station where they caused further havoc of a spectacular and enjoy-able kind.

These were perhaps not ideal conditions under which to

learn how to drive an engine, especially as the whole thing was carried out under shell-fire; and all we really knew for certain about Norman's capabilities as an engine-driver was that every single locomotive with which he had been associated had become scrap metal in a matter of minutes. Still, he is a very determined and a very methodical chap, and there seemed no harm in letting him have a go. So early in the morning we made our way to the railway station, just in time for the first air-raid of the day. Except for occasional parties of refugees and stragglers from the Greek army the station was deserted. There were two excellent reasons for this. First of all there were no trains running, so there was no point in anybody going there anyhow. Secondly, the station was practically the only thing left in the ruins of Larissa that was worth bombing; we had ten air raids altogether before we left in the afternoon, and they always had a go at the station.

The first thing we had to do was to get steam up in a railway engine. There were plenty of these about but all except two had been rendered unserviceable by the Luftwaffe. We started work on the bigger of the two. After having a quick look round, Norman explained to us that one of the most popular and probably in the long run the soundest of all methods of making steam was by boiling water, but, he said, we might have to devise some alternative formula as the water mains had been cut by bombs and there was very little coal to be found. However, in the long run we got together enough of these two more or less essential ingredients, and all was going well when one of the few really large bombs that came our way blew a hole in the track just outside the shed we were working in, thus, as it were, locking the stable door before we had been able to steal the horse. Greatly disgusted, we transferred our attention to the other sound engine.

There were more air-raids, and it came on to rain, and two Greek deserters stole my car, and altogether things did not look very hopeful, especially when somebody pointed out that there was now only one undamaged and navigable set of tracks leading out of the battered marshalling yard. But the needle on the pressure-gauge in the cabin of our engine was rising slowly, and at last, whistling excitedly, the ancient machine got under way. It was a majestic sight, and it would have been even more majestic if she had not gone backwards instead of forwards.

It was at this point that a certain gap in Norman's education as an engine-driver became evident. The sergeant in the 4th Hussars had taught him how to start a locomotive and how to launch it on a career of self-destruction; but Norman's early training in how to stop an engine had been confined entirely to making it run violently into a lot of other rolling stock. We trotted anxiously along the cinders, hanging, so to speak, on to Norman's stirrup leathers. "Do you know how to stop?" we shouted. "Not yet," replied Norman, a trifle testily. But he soon found out and presently mastered the knack of making the engine go forwards as well as backwards, and we steamed rather incredulously northwards towards the siding where the ammunition trains lay.

We chose the bigger of the two. It consisted of twenty-six trucks containing 120 tons of ammunition and 150 tons of petrol. It was not what you might call an ideally balanced cargo from our point of view, and nobody particularly wanted the petrol, but the train was made up like that and we had to lump it.

It really was rather a proud moment when we steamed back through Larissa with this enormous train clattering along behind us, and out into the broad plain of Thessaly. Norman drove, the stoker was Oliver Barstow—a young officer in the Royal Horse Artillery who was killed a few days later—

and Guardsman Loveday and I, armed with our only Tommy gun, prepared to engage any hostile aircraft who might be so foolhardy as to come within range. It was a lovely evening, and we all felt tremendously pleased with ourselves. Driving a train, once you had got the beastly thing started, seemed to be extraordinarily easy. No steering, no gear-changing, no problems of navigation, no flat tyres, none of those uncomfortable suspicions that perhaps after all you ought to have taken that last turning to the left. There's nothing in it, we told each other. I am afraid we were suffering from what Stalin once called "dizziness from success."

Almost as soon as we had left Larissa we had begun to climb up a long, gentle slope; and we had only done about five miles when the needle on the pressure gauge began slowly but firmly to fall. We stoked like mad. Norman pulled, pushed and twiddled the various devices on what we quite incorrectly called the dashboard. Pressure continued to fall and the train went slower and slower. At last it stopped altogether. "We'd better get out" said Norman, "and have a look at the injector-sprockets." He may not actually have said "injector-sprockets" but anyhow it was some technical term which meant nothing to us and may not have meant a very great deal to him. It was at this point that we realised that the train had not merely stopped but was beginning to run slowly backwards down the hill. The thought of free-wheeling backwards into Larissa was distasteful to all of us. In the hurry of departure we had had no time to organise our ten brakesmen, who were all confined in the guard's van instead of being dispersed along the train so that they could operate the brakes on individual goods wagons. There was only one thing to do. I leapt off the engine and ran back down the train as fast as I could, like an old lady running for a bus: jumped on the back of the nearest goods van, swarmed up a little ladder on to its roof and feverishly turned the wheel which put the brake on. The train continued to go backwards, but it seemed to have stopped gathering speed and at last, after I had repeated this operation several times, it came reluctantly to a stop.

We were really getting a great deal of fun out of this train. We had got a tremendous kick out of starting it, and now we were scarcely less elated at having brought it to a standstill. But we had to face the facts, and the main fact was that as engine-drivers, though we had no doubt some excellent qualities—originality, determination, cheerfulness, and so on —we were open to the serious criticism that we did not seem to be able to drive our engine very far. A run of five miles, with a small discount for going backwards unexpectedly, is not much to show for a hard day's work. At this point, moreover, it suddenly began to look as if we were going to lose our precious train altogether. As we tinkered away at the engine, the air grew loud with an expected but none the less unwelcome noise, and a number of enemy bombers could be seen marching through the sky towards us. We were a very conspicuous object in the middle of that empty plain and I quickly gave orders for the ten men in the guard's van to go and take cover 500 yards from the train. In point of fact there was no cover to take, but they trotted off with alacrity and sat down round a small tree about the size of a big gooseberry bush in the middle distance. We couldn't very well leave the engine because the fire might have gone out (or anyhow we thought it might) and we should have had to start all over again.

But if we had our troubles the enemy, as so often happens, had his too. The bombers were obviously interested in us, but it soon became equally obvious that they had no bombs, having wasted all theirs on the ruins of Larissa earlier in the day. They still, however, had their machine-guns and three or four of the aircraft proceeded to attack us, coming in very low one after the other. But they all made the same mistake, which they might not have made if we ourselves had taken evasive action and left the train. They all attacked the engine, round which they could see signs of life, instead of flying up and down the twenty-odd wagons full of petrol and H.E. and spraying them with bullets, which could hardly have failed to produce spectacular results. They concentrated on putting the engine out of action; and the engine, as we ourselves were just beginning to realise, was out of action already, all the water in the boiler having somehow disappeared.

We used the engine in much the same way as one uses a grouse-butt. Whichever side the attack was coming from we got the other side. The flying-machine, making a terrible noise and blazing away with its machine-guns, swept down on us and as it roared overhead—much bigger, much more malevolent but not really very much higher than the average grouse—we pooped off at it with our Tommy gun, to which the German rear-gunner replied with a burst that kicked up the dust a hundred yards away or more. It got rather silly after a bit. I am quite sure we never hit the Luftwaffe, and the only damage the Luftwaffe did to us was to make a hole in a map somebody had left in the cab. And one of the things about driving a train is that you don't need a map to do it with. They gave it up quite soon—it was getting late anyhow—and went home to Bulgaria. We climbed back into our engine again and as I looked at our only casualty—the map, torn by an explosive bullet and covered with coal dust —I couldn't help rather envying the Luftwaffe, who almost certainly believed that they had succeeded in doing what they set out to do. It was only too obvious that we had not. Night fell, and it was fairly cold.

Then, all of a sudden out of the darkness, another train appeared. It was full of Australian gunners whose guns were supposed to have come on by road. They towed us back to the next station. Here we picked up a good engine with a Greek driver and set off for the south. It was ideal weather all next day—pouring rain and low cloud—and we never saw a German aeroplane at all. Forty-eight hours after we had started work on this unlikely project we reached our—or rather the ammunition's—destination. It was a place called Amphykleion and here I formally handed over the train—26 coaches, 150 tons of petrol, 120 tons of ammunition—to the supply people. Everyone was delighted with it. "This really will make a difference," they said. We felt childishly pleased. The sun shone, it was a lovely morning. And this marked improvement in the weather made it comparatively easy for a small force of German dive-bombers, a few hours later, to dispose of the train and all its contents with a terrible finality.

PETER FLEMING

102. DRIVER GIMBERT, G.C.

IT happened in the small hours of June 2, 1944. A March driver, Benjamin Gimbert by name, was rostered to take a trainload of bombs from March to Whitemoor by way of Ely and Ipswich. He had forty 500 lb. bombs in the first wagon, seventy-four more in the second, a load of detonators in the third, and after that some forty-eight more wagons all filled with high explosives. For an engine they had one of the War Department eight-coupled locomotives, one of the ugliest creatures that ever ran on a British railway.

They started at 12.15 A.M. and made their slow way to Ely, through the Junction, and then on by single line through Soham to Fordham. All went well until they were approaching Soham, when the driver looked out and saw that the first wagon was on fire. He knew well enough what the train contained, and he and his mate might just have had time to get down and run for it. But they did not choose to do so for they were not that kind of men. He stopped the train carefully, well short of the station, and sent his fireman to uncouple the burning wagon from the rest of the train, remembering to tell him to take a coal hammer with him in case the coupling was too hot to touch. This was successfully done, and driver Gimbert then proceeded with his blazing wagon into the station, intending to take it some distance along the line, where it would be well clear of all buildings, to uncouple it from the engine there, while he and his mate hoped to be able to take the engine on to Fordham. The signal-box at Soham is on the station, and the signalman, seeing that something was wrong, came down on to the platform as his duty was. The driver hailed him, "Sailor, have you got anything between here and Fordham. Where's the mail?" That question was never answered: at the moment of asking it the wagon exploded. It blew the engine's tender to pieces, killed the signalman and the fireman, and Gimbert himself recovered consciousness lying on the far platform badly injured. Virtually every window in Soham was smashed and the station itself completely wrecked. The crater underneath the wagon was fifteen feet deep and sixty-six feet wide. For this the driver and fireman received the George Cross, the fireman, alas, posthumously; and there is of course no doubt at all that their courage and resource saved the town of Soham, for had that whole train exploded, as it must have done if the blazing wagon had not been uncoupled and drawn well away from the rest, there could have been nothing left of the town. One hardly knows what to admire more, the courage or the coolness, but—as what has already been said shows—there was hardly any driver who would not under the same circumstances have acted in exactly the same way. To-day the new Soham station carries a memorial plaque in honour of Fireman Nightall and Driver Gimbert, with the inscription, "The devotion to duty of these brave men saved the town of Soham from grave destruction."

CANON ROGER LLOYD

103. THE GREAT FREEZE-UP

THERE was one day in the blizzard winter of 1946–7 when even the humble coal train came into its own. When every electric power station was down to its last few bags of coal, and the weather was so appalling that every truck of coal shifted from the pit mouth represented prodigies of endurance on the part of many men, a little crowd of passengers were waiting for the 8.15 A.M. from Amersham to Baker Street. It was very late and they were bitterly cold, stamping their feet on an ice-clogged platform. At last the signal went down, and hopefulness warmed them a little. The engine was spotted in the distance, and the passengers made ready to board the train. But as it came near they saw that after all it was a freight, and not for them. The engine, an old Great Central 0-8-0, came slowly through. Icicles hung from the frames and running boards, and dirty snow covered the back half of the tender. Behind it were fifty loaded coal wagons, each one filled with lumps of black coal frozen solidly together and covered with snow. The waiting passengers regarded it, and then somebody began to cheer it as it passed, and one by one they all joined in. They knew how desperately that coal was wanted, and perhaps at that moment they had a vision of the aching backs and half-frozen fingers up in Yorkshire, of the shunters and linesmen working long hours of overtime out in the blizzard, and of the watchful skill in the control rooms which had found the way out of whatever crisis it was which had caused them to send it to London on an unwonted path down the old Metropolitan line.

CANON ROGER LLOYD

The Communication Cord

104. OUT OF TOUCH

Sir,

I take the liberty of calling your attention to the following statement. . . . We left York at 4 o'clock yesterday afternoon (Sept. 30) by the express train, which runs daily between London and Edinburgh, the train consisting of a luggage van next the engine, and three first-class carriages. We had scarcely passed the Thirsk station when we—the occupants of the last carriage—were alarmed by being violently jolted in our seats, and in a few seconds we found ourselves off the line, our speed at the time, according to the engine-driver's own statement, exceeding 50 miles an hour. Our first impulse was to endeavour to make the guard aware of our danger by shouting, but this attempt proving utterly fruitless, we lay down with outstretched legs and prepared for the worst. Most providentially, however, the engine-driver, perceiving, as he said, a "jumping motion" on the engine, stopped the train with as little delay as possible; but not before we had been dragged along the embankment for three quarters of a mile, and the tire of one of the wheels had ploughed up the flooring of the centre compartment of the carriage.

As this accident was not attended with fatal, or even serious, results, the probability is that no notice will be taken of it, unless you, Sir, give it publicity, for the sake of impressing upon the railway authorities the absolute necessity of establishing some means of communication between the passengers and the guard of the train; who in this instance was seated inside the luggage van next the engine, both out of hearing and out of sight of all the carriages, unless he chanced to look out of the window, when he could only see the adjoining carriage. . . .

A. KEPPEL MACDONALD
Scots Fusilier Guards
Kirkley-hall, Newcastle-on-Tyne, Oct. 1, 1847

105. THE GAMP OF PROPRIETY

A CLERGYMAN found himself alone in a compartment of an express train in which were also a young lady and a man, both total strangers to him. Shortly after the train started the man began to give unmistakable indications of something wrong. He made no attempt at any violence on either of his fellow passengers, but he was noisy, and presently he proceeded to disrobe himself and otherwise to indulge in antics which were even more indecent than they were extraordinary. The poor clergyman,—a respected incumbent of the established church returning to the bosom of his family,—was in a most distressing situation. At first he attempted remonstrance. This, however, proved worse than unavailing, and there was nothing for it but to have recourse to his umbrella, behind the sheltering cover of which he protected the modesty of the young lady, while over its edges he himself from time to time effected observations through an apparently interminable journey of forty and more miles.

C. F. ADAMS

106. E PERICOLOSO SPORGERSI

ON one occasion I went home from Greece overland and was travelling by train from Salonika to Nish in Servia to catch the Orient Express. About eleven in the morning we were running down a pretty stream valley not far from Nish when suddenly the conductor entered our compartment and pulled down the blinds on the side towards the stream. There was an Englishman in the carriage who lived in Belgrade, so I said to him, "Tell this fellow that we do not want the blinds down." The conductor turned to me and said, "I spik Inglese. I have been in New York. I will tell you. Some months ago—four months—six months—there come an Ingleseman by this train and he look out of ze window and he see a girl bathing in zat river, and he get out at ze next station, and he make ze acquaintance of zat girl, and he marry her. And now whenever zis train come all ze girls of ze village do bathe in ze river, and ze control has ordered that when we go by zis stream ze blinds shall be pulled down."

R. B. GRUNDY

107. INFECTIOUS INSANITY

SOME years ago, the driver and stoker of the express train running from Brussels to Antwerp, normally a journey of less than an hour, were attacked by infectious insanity. The points had to be altered for them all over Belgium, and the signals raised, and they tore from end to end of the country, round and round until the steam was exhausted and the train ran to a standstill. Most of the passengers were removed in hysterics. A friend who was on board tells me it was the most exhausting day of sightseeing he has ever known.

"ATTICUS" IN THE SUNDAY TIMES

108. MAL DE TRAIN

PEOPLE who find it necessary to vomit whilst in a railway carriage should discreetly use their hats; this would come naturally to anyone properly brought up.

FROM A LETTER IN PICTURE POST, 1952

109. JOURNEY WITH A MANIAC

ON Friday last I took the 10.35 A.M. train from Lime Street in a third-class carriage, my destination being Chester. At Edge Hill Station the prisoner and another man, whom I afterwards understood to be the prisoner's father, got into the same compartment. . . .

After we had passed over Runcorn bridge and through the station, I perceived the prisoner make a start, and looking toward him saw a white-hafted knife in his hand, about five inches long, with the blade open. He held it in his right hand in a menacing manner. Drawing his left hand along the edge of the blade, he said, "This will have to go into some ———." At that moment he looked at me across the carriage; he was on his feet in an instant, and looking across to me, he said, "You ———, this will have to go into you," and made a bound toward me. The other jumped up and tried to prevent him. The prisoner threw him away; he made a plunge at my throat. I caught his wrist just as he advanced, and struggled with him, still holding fast to his wrist with both hands. We fell over and under one another two or three times, and eventually he overpowered me. I had fallen on my side on the seat, but still retained my hold upon his wrist. While lying in that position he held the knife down to within an inch of my throat. I called to the other man to hold the prisoner's hand back which contained the knife, and by that means he saved my life. I was growing powerless, and as the other man restrained the prisoner from using the knife, I jerked myself out of his grasp, and knocked the knife out of the prisoner's hand with my left hand.

The prisoner eluded the grip of his father, and falling on his knees began to seek for his knife. Failing to find the knife, he was instantly on his feet, and made a spring upon me. . . . We had then a very long and desperate struggle, when he overpowered me and pinned me in a corner of the compartment. At last he got my right thumb into his mouth, holding my hand to steady it with both his hands while he bit it. With a great effort he then bit my thumb off, clean to the bone. I had no glove on that hand. I called to the other man to help me, but he seemed stupefied. He called two or three times to the prisoner, "Leave the poor man alone. The poor man has done thee no harm." Though sitting within nine inches of my knees he rendered me no help.

When the prisoner bit my thumb off, he held it in his mouth; he pushed his head through the glass, spat the thumb into his hand and flung it through the window. I then stood up and put my left hand in my pocket, took out my purse and cried out: "If it is money you want take all I have." He made a grab at the purse and flung it through the window, on the same side as the thumb was thrown out. From this act I inferred that I was struggling with a maniac. I retreated to the other end of the compartment, holding the other man between me and the prisoner, but he passed the other man by jumping over the seat and again got hold of me. Then he forced his head through the other window, breaking the glass, and, loosing me for a moment, with his fists smashed the remaining glass in the window. Addressing me he said:

"You ——, you will have to go over"; at the same time he flung both his arms round my waist. I put my leg behind his and threw him on his back. I called upon the other man to help me and he did so.

We held him down for some time, but he overpowered us and flung us back some distance. He then laid hold of my travelling rug and threw it through the window. Laying his hand on the bottom of the window he cried out, "Here goes," and made a leap through the window. I and the other man instantly laid hold of his legs as he was falling over. I got my four fingers into his right shoe, and, his father assisting me, we held him through the window, hanging head downward for about half a mile. I then fainted, and as I was losing my hold on his heels I have some recollection that the prisoner's father lost his hold at the same time, and I can't say what happened afterward.

EVIDENCE IN COURT, 1876

Journeys in Fact and Fancy

I. FACT

110. THE SEEING EYES

THE weather after Exeter got worse and worse—the wind began to bluster, the lightning changed from summer gleams to spiteful forks, and the roll of thunder was almost continuous; and by the time we reached Beam Bridge the storm was at such terrible purpose that the faithful guard wrapped me up in his waterproof and lifted me, literally, into the shed which served as a station. In like manner, when the train was ready, he lifted me high and dry into a first-c ass carriage, in which were two elderly, cosy, friendly-looking gentlemen, evidently fellows in friendship as well as in travel. The old Great Western carriages were double, held eight persons, four in each compartment, and there was a glass door between; which was on this occasion left open. One old gentleman sat with his face to the horses (so to speak) on my side, and one in the inside corner, opposite to me exactly. When I had taken off my cloak and smoothed my plumes, and generally settled myself, I looked up to see the most wonderful eyes I ever saw, steadily, luminously, clairvoyantly, kindly, paternally looking at me. The hat was over the forehead, the mouth and chin buried in the brown velvet coat collar of the brown greatcoat. I looked at him, wondering if my grandfather's eyes had been like those. I should have described them as the most "seeing" eyes I had ever seen. My father had often spoken of my grandfather's eyes, as being capable of making a hundred ugly faces handsome; and the peasants used to say: "Divil a sowl could tell a lie to his Riverence's Worship's *eyes*." (He was a magistrate as well as a parson.) My opposite neighbour's seemed much of this sort.

Well, we went on, and the storm went on more and more, until we reached Bristol; to wait ten minutes. My old gentleman rubbed the side window with his coat cuff, in vain; attacked the centre window, again in vain, so blurred and blotted was it with the torrents of rain! A moment's hesitation, and then:

"Young lady, would you mind my putting down this window?"

"Oh, no, not at all."

"You may be drenched, you know."

"Never mind, sir."

Immediately, down goes the window, out go the old gentleman's head and shoulders, and there they stay for I suppose nearly nine minutes. Then he drew them in, and I said:

"Oh, please let me look."

"Now you *will* be drenched"; but he half-opened the window for me to see. Such a sight, such a chaos of elemental and artificial lights and noises I never saw or heard, or expect to see or hear. He drew up the window as we moved on, and then leant back with closed eyes for I dare say ten minutes; then opened them and said:

"Well?"

I said: "I've been drenched, but it's worth it."

He nodded and smiled, and again took to his steady but quite inoffensive perusing of my face, and presently said it was a bad night for one so young and alone. He had not seen me at Exeter.

"No, I got in at Plymouth."

"Plymouth!"

"Yes." I then said I could only save my friends trouble and anxiety by travelling up that night, and told them simply how it came to pass. Then, except a little joke when we were going through a long tunnel (then the terror of "elegant females"), silence until Swindon, but always the speculative steady look. There we all got out and I got some tea and biscuits. When we were getting in (the storm by then over) they asked me if I had got some refreshment, and when I said tea, my friend with the eyes said:

"Tea! Poor stuff; you should have had soup."

I said tea was more refreshing, as I had not had anything since eight the previous morning. We all laughed, and I found the two cosy friends had had something more "comfortable" than tea, and speedily fell into slumber, while I watched the dawn and oncoming brightness of one of the loveliest June mornings that had ever visited the earth.

At six o'clock we steamed into Paddington station, and I had signalled a porter before my friends roused themselves. They were very kind—could they do anything to help me? where had I to go to? "Hammersmith: that was a long drive." Then they took off their hats, and went off arm in arm. . . .

The next year, I think, going to the Academy, I turned at once, as I always did, to see what Turners there were.

Imagine my feelings:

"RAIN, STEAM, AND SPEED,
GREAT WESTERN RAILWAY, JUNE THE —, 1843."

I had found out who the "seeing" eyes belonged to! As I stood looking at the picture, I heard a mawkish voice behind me say:

"There now, just look at that; ain't it *just* like Turner? Whoever saw such a ridiculous conglomeration?"

I turned very quietly round and said:

"*I* did; I was in the train that night, and it is perfectly and wonderfully true"; and walked quietly away.

MRS. JOHN SIMON

III. DAWN

(From the train between Bologna and Milan, second class)

Opposite me two Germans snore and sweat.
  Through sullen swirling gloom we jolt and roar.
We have been here for ever: even yet
  A dim watch tells two hours, two æons, more.
The windows are tight-shut and slimy-wet
  With a night's fœtor. There are two hours more;
Two hours to dawn and Milan; two hours yet.
  Opposite me two Germans sweat and snore. . . .

One of them wakes, and spits, and sleeps again.
  The darkness shivers. A wan light through the rain
Strikes on our faces, drawn and white. Somewhere
  A new day sprawls; and, inside, the foul air
Is chill, and damp, and fouler than before. . . .
Opposite me two Germans sweat and snore.

RUPERT BROOKE

112. SNOWBOUND IN THE ORIENT EXPRESS

On Tuesday, January 29, at 10.45 A.M., we left Victoria for Constantinople, a journey which usually takes four days and three nights.

By Thursday morning we were past Zagreb, in Serbia, but already some hours late. After Sofia, where we were about eight hours late, we left ordinary conditions and entered the realms of "Wellsian" romance. Snow was falling heavily out of an inky black sky, and nature was the only force apparent in that world of bleak loneliness. Somewhere, about 8 P.M., we pulled up at a spot which we afterwards discovered was Cerkezköy. The wind and snow, which had both been on the increase, were now tremendous—so bad indeed that it was considered undesirable to start the train till the storm abated somewhat, but this proved a vain hope. By 2 A.M. nearly all the pipes on the weather side of the train were frozen, in spite of the strenuous efforts of the train's personnel to keep the heating apparatus going!

I wish I could describe this blizzard. A blizzard to most of us means a shrieking wind, a thing of tumult and fury. Here was silence—one felt, rather than heard, the impenetrable mass of snow driving over us at a terrific speed. In that train we felt like a microcosm of civilisation helpless under the rage of natural forces, and civilisation seemed a very small and futile thing. With terrible monotony the blizzard went on, hour after hour, with a hum like a suppressed dynamo, a faint hissing and sighing note hidden within it, giving an awful impression of relentless power, cruelty and ruthlessness. We were literally at the mercy of the elements, in the centre of a plain, where nothing sheltered us or impeded the steady onrush of that elemental fury. When the blizzard passed, at the end of the third day, it was succeeded by an unutterable silence in which one listened with straining ears for any sound of life. On the second day of the storm a woman, carrying a child of two, one of a party from the village which had been caught at the station when the storm commenced, tried to get back. They described how, almost immediately after leaving the shelter of the building, the woman and child were whisked away like a feather, and though they searched for as long as they were able, nothing more was seen of them, till they were found two days later, frozen to death.

At this time the elemental necessities of food and warmth were all we thought of. Everything else seemed unreal and part of another world. The actual storm had lasted from Friday night, February 1, till nightfall of Monday 4. On Tuesday morning we saw the sun for an hour or two, but the intense cold and bitter wind continued. The respite was most welcome and enabled us to take stock of our position and to begin to take an intelligent interest in each other; we *were* a mixed bag: Two Englishmen and one Englishwoman; two Germans and one German woman; two French women and one Frenchman; two Danes, one American, one Italian, one Swiss, one Turk, one Armenian, and one Japanese— seventeen people representing ten different nationalities. Not much doubt about its being an International train! And we soon became a fairly harmonious League of Nations.

The most reassuring fact was that Cerkezköy, where we found ourselves, was a depot, which meant there was a stock of coal and that water was obtainable, and there was a village about a mile away where we soon discovered we could get bread, eggs and some chickens.

The telegraph lines had been out of action, but after a time intermittent communication was established with Constantinople; the news that came through, however, was not encouraging! The whole country was snowbound and paralysed; Constantinople itself was in a bad way—and the line appeared to be blocked in six or seven places. Various rumours reached us. One said that the Turkish army had been mobilized and was being sent to dig us out! This we afterwards heard had been attempted, but owing to the excessive suffering endured by the troops from frostbite, and the difficulties of transport and feeding, the attempt had to be abandoned.

For nearly the whole of the eleven days at Cerkezköy, the temperature in the train was hardly ever more than three or four degrees above freezing during the day time and at night it would go to 25 or 30 degrees below. One very curious thing that happened was that the mineral-water bottles in the restaurant car froze, forcing the metal stoppers off, the water freezing as it rose like a candle to a height of seven or eight inches in a perfectly round and smooth column. We managed to get through the time somehow, using the restaurant car, the only one in which the pipes had not burst, as a general living-room. We played bridge, read, and did crossword puzzles in any of the newspapers we had left. For light we were dependent on a limited supply of candles. Monday, February 11, was a red-letter day. The snow-plough which had been trying to reach us worked its way through. They had had a pretty bad time, were quite exhausted, and had suffered intensely from the cold. They assured us, however, that they would have us into Constantinople some time that night, but it sounded too good to be true.

About 7 P.M. they were ready to attempt the start. The plough, driven by two engines, would proceed a few miles and then signal back for us to come on. All went well till about 10 P.M., by which time we were some 25 miles nearer Constantinople; there we stuck till 4 A.M., when at last news came back that the snow-plough was again stuck, two miles from the next station, that was some twelve miles ahead of where we then were. This was rather heart-breaking, and the morning of Tuesday the 12th was a cheerless business. Here we were, at a spot called Chatalja, another 18 inches of snow had fallen during the night, and the news was, that there was no food, not even water, and that the village of Chatalja, three miles away, was itself very badly off for food! This was, without doubt, our most miserable day.

At about 5 P.M. good news arrived; the snow-plough, pushed by four engines, had forced a passage through the worst drift, and the way was once more declared open and hope revived. When we again began to move forward, the suppressed excitement became intense; should we or should we not get there! If we could only keep moving, a couple of hours would do it. *It did.* At 7.30, on the night of the 12th, we arrived in Constantinople. An enormous crowd clapped frantically as the train slowly pulled into the station. No amount of applause would have induced us to give an encore.

MAJOR A. F. CUSTANCE
King's Messenger

113. TRANS-SIBERIAN EXPRESS

As I settled down in my compartment, and the train pulled out through shoddy suburbs into a country clothed in birch and fir, the unreal rhythm of train-life was resumed as though it had never been broken. The nondescript smell of the upholstery, the unrelenting rattle of our progress, the tall glass of weak tea in its metal holder, the unshaven jowls and fatuous but friendly smile of the little attendant who brought it—all these unmemorable components of a former routine, suddenly resurrected, blotted out the interim between this journey and the last. The inconsequent comedy of two years, with the drab or coloured places, the cities and the forests, where it had been played, became for a moment as though it had never been. This small, timeless, moving cell I recognized as my home and my doom. I felt as if I had always been on the Trans-Siberian Express.

The dining-car was certainly unchanged. On each table there still ceremoniously stood two opulent black bottles of some unthinkable wine, false pledges of conviviality. They were never opened, and rarely dusted. They may contain ink, they may contain the elixir of life. I do not know. I doubt if anyone does.

Lavish but faded paper frills still clustered coyly round the pots of paper flowers, from whose sad petals the dust of two continents perpetually threatened the specific gravity of the soup. The lengthy and trilingual menu had not been revised; 75 per cent of the dishes were still apocryphal, all the prices were exorbitant. The cruet, as before, was of interest rather to the geologist than to the gourmet. Coal dust from the Donetz Basin, tiny flakes of granite from the Urals, sand whipped by the wind all the way from the Gobi Desert—what a fascinating story that salt-cellar could have told under the microscope! Nor was there anything different about the attendants. They still sat in huddled cabal at the far end of the car, conversing in low and disillusioned tones, while the *chef du train*, a potent gnome-like man, played on his abacus a slow significant tattoo. Their surliness went no deeper than the grime upon their faces; they were always ready to be amused by one's struggles with the language or the cooking. Sign-language they interpreted with more eagerness than apprehension: as when my desire for a hard-boiled egg—no easy request, when you come to think of it, to make in panto-mime—was fulfilled, three-quarters of an hour after it had been expressed, by the appearance of a whole roast fowl.

The only change of which I was aware was in my stable-companion. Two years ago it had been a young Australian, a man much preoccupied with the remoter contingencies of travel. "Supposing," he would muse, "the train breaks down, will there be danger of attack by wolves?" When he undressed he panted fiercely, as though wrestling with the invisible Fiend; he had a plaintive voice, and on his lips the words "nasal douche" (the mere sound of Siberia had given him a cold) had the saddest cadence you can imagine. This time it was a young Russian, about whom I remember nothing at all. Nor is this surprising, for I never found out anything about him. He spoke no English, and I spoke hardly any Russian. A phrase-book bought in Moscow failed to bridge the gap between us. An admirable compilation in many ways, it did not, I discovered, equip one for casual conversation with a stranger. There was a certain petulance, a touch of the imperious and exorbitant, about such observations as: "Show me the manager, the assistant manager, the water closet, Lenin's Tomb," and "Please to bring me tea, coffee, beer, wodka, cognac, Caucasian red wine, Caucasian white wine." Besides, a lot of the questions, like "Can you direct me to the Palace of the Soviets?" and "Why must I work for a World Revolution?" were not the sort of things I wanted to ask him; and most of the plain statements of fact—such as "I am an American engineer who loves Russia" and "I wish to study Architecture, Medicine, Banking under the best teachers, please"—would have been misleading. I did not want to mislead him.

So for two days we grinned and nodded and got out of each other's way and watched each other incuriously, in silence. On the second day he left the train, and after that I had the compartment to myself. . . .

Most men, though not the best men, are happiest when the question "What shall I do?" is supererogatory. (Hence the common and usually just contention that "My schooldays were the happiest days of my life.") That is why I like the Trans-Siberian Railway. You lie in your berth, justifiably inert. Past the window plains crawl and forests flicker. The sun shines weakly on an empty land. The piles of birch logs by the permanent way—silver on the outside, black where the damp butts show—give the anomalous illusion that there has been a frost. There is always a magpie in sight.

You have nothing to look at, but no reason to stop looking. You are living in a vacuum, and at last you have to invent some absurdly artificial necessity for getting up: "fifteen magpies from now," or "next time the engine whistles." For you are inwardly afraid that without some self-discipline to give it a pattern this long period of suspended animation will permanently affect your character for the worse.

So in the end you get up, washing perfunctorily in the little dark confessional which you share with the next compartment, and in the basin for which the experienced traveller brings his own plug, because the Russians, for some reason connected—strangely enough—with religion, omit to furnish these indispensable adjuncts to a careful toilet.

Then, grasping your private pot of marmalade, you lurch along to the dining-car. It is now eleven o'clock, and the dining-car is empty. You order tea and bread, and make without appetite a breakfast which is more than sufficient for your needs. The dining-car is almost certainly stuffy, but you have ceased to notice this. The windows are always shut, either because the weather is cold, or because it is warm and dry and therefore dusty. (Not, of course, that the shutting of them excludes the dust. Far from it. But it is at least a gesture; it is the best that can be done.)

After that you wander back to your compartment. The *provodnik* has transformed your bed into a seat, and perhaps you hold with him some foolish conversation, in which the rudiments of three languages are prostituted in an endeavour to compliment each other on their simultaneous mastery.

Then you sit down and read. You read and read and read. There are no distractions, no interruptions, no temptations to get up and do something else; there is nothing else to do. You read as you have never read before.

And so the day passes. If you are wise you shun the regulation meal at three o'clock, which consists of five courses not easily to be identified, and during which the car is crowded and the windows blurred with steam. I had brought with me from London biscuits and potted meat and cheese; and he is a fool who does not take at least some victuals of his own. But as a matter of fact, what with the airless atmosphere and the lack of exercise, you don't feel hungry on the Trans-Siberian Railway. A pleasant lassitude, a sense almost of disembodiment, descends on you, and the food in the dining-car which, though seldom really bad, is never appetizing and sometimes scarce, hardly attracts that vigorous criticism which it would on a shorter journey.

At the more westerly stations—there are perhaps three stops of twenty minutes every day—you pace the platforms vigorously, in a conscientious British way. But gradually this practice is abandoned. As you are drawn farther into Asia, old fetishes lose their power. It becomes harder and harder to persuade yourself that you feel a craving for exercise, and indeed you almost forget that you ought to feel this craving. At first you are alarmed, for this is the East, the notorious East, where white men go to pieces; you fear that you are losing your grip, that you are going native. But you do nothing about it, and soon your conscience ceases to prick and it seems quite natural to stand limply in the sunlight, owlish, frowsty, and immobile, like everybody else.

At last evening comes. The sun is setting somewhere far back along the road that you have travelled. A slanting light always lends intimacy to a landscape, and this Siberia, flecked darkly by the tapering shadows of trees, seems a place at once more friendly and more mysterious than the naked non-committal flats of noon. Your eyes are tired, and you put down your book. Against the grey and creeping distances outside, memory and imagination stage in their turn the struggles of the past and of the future. For the first time loneliness descends, and you sit examining its implications until you find Siberia vanished and the grimy window offering nothing save your own face, foolish, indistinct, and as likely as not unshaved. You adjourn to the dining-car, for eggs.

PETER FLEMING

114. ON THE FLYING SCOTSMAN

"WELL, did you get your ride on the engine?"

"Rather!"

"What was it like?"

"Marvellous, simply marvellous—a jolly sight more marvellous than you'd expect and yet in some ways quite the opposite."

I got to King's Cross about 9.30 (wasn't going to risk being late) and, after a cup of tea and a sandwich, I ventured into the guard's van of the train, at which the guard, looking very spruce, had just arrived with bag and flags and what not, and said: "I say, good morning, look here, it's like this; I've got this engine pass to Grantham." "Oh, have you?" "Yes, and, I say, can I leave my bag in here till I come off the engine?" No objection to that, so I stepped back on to the platform and there I saw Mr. Sparke, the District Locomotive Superintendent, and a friend of his. Mr. Sparke had very kindly come to introduce me to Mr. Young of Newcastle, the driver of the engine, and his friend kindly presented me with a nice clean swab to wipe my hands on from time to time. (Forgot all about it afterwards, but kept it as a memento!) The engine, No. 2582 of Newcastle, then backed in and I was introduced to Mr. Young—very grand and important and an object of curiosity to the group of enthusiasts on the platform (I mean me, not Mr. Young).

I was born beside the railway at Brighton, and I spent most of my childhood examining and drawing locomotives, and what surprised me now was, first, how little things had changed in fundamentals since I was a child 35 years ago and, second, how simple in idea the mechanism of steam engines still is. A detail that struck me immediately was that the throttle lever on the L.N.E.R. engine was worked by pulling it upwards towards you whereas on the engines of my Brighton childhood it was worked by a lever at right angles to the axis of the boiler.

The remaining few minutes were spent in explanations of the brake apparatus, steam pressure required—the names of this and that and then someone called up from outside: "right you are" and I gathered that it must be exactly 10.0. The engine was driven from the right-hand side, so I was given the piano-stool or perch on the left side, with one foot on a pail (a quite ordinary household-looking pail) and the other dangling. Up to this time the fireman had been doing various odd jobs about the place. He now shut (if you can call it shutting, for it only about half covered the gap) the iron door between engine and tender, and Mr. Young, having made a suitable response to the man outside who had shouted "right you are," pulled up the handle (both hands to the job and not too much at a time—a mouthful, so to say, for a start, to let her feel the weight) and, well, we simply started forward. It's as simple as that. I mean it *looks* as simple as that.

And, immediately, the fireman started shovelling coal. I shouted some apology to him for taking his seat. I could not hear his reply. It was probably to say that he had no time for seats. He shovelled in about 6 shovelsful; then, after a few seconds' pause, another half dozen—a few seconds' pause and then six or more shovels and so on practically without stopping the whole time. What strikes you about this, even more than the colossal labour of the thing and the great skill with which he distributes the coal in the fire and his unerring aim in throwing a pretty big shovelful of coal through a not very large opening, what strikes you is the extraordinary primitive nature of the job. You stand in a space about as big as a hearthrug spread out longways to the fire and you take a shovelful of coal out of a hole at one end and throw it through a hole in the other end—spilling a bit every time. You go on doing this for hours. Your attention must be as great as your skill and strength. You must watch the pressure gauges and you must watch the state of the fire at the same time. And your only relaxations are when, on entering tunnels or passing stations, you give a tug at the whistle handle and when, on a signal from the driver, you let down the water scoop to take up water from the trough between the rails (which occurs every hundred miles or so). And talking of primitive things, look at the whistle handle! It is a round ring on the end of a wire (there is one on each side of the cab). It dangles down about a foot from the roof. When the train is travelling fast you have to make a bit of a grab for it as it is never in the same place for two seconds together. On receiving a nod of acquiescence from Mr. Young, I pulled the handle myself as we approached Peterborough, and again as we went, at reduced speed, through the station itself. (My first pull was but a timid little shriek, but my second was, it seemed to me, a long bold blast.)

But don't imagine I'm complaining or sneering about this primitiveness. It's no more primitive or less venerable than sawing with a hand-saw or ploughing with a horse plough. I only think that it's surprising how these primitive methods persist. Here we were on an engine of the most powerful kind in the world, attached to one of the most famous of all travelling hotels—the string of coaches called The Flying Scotsman—with its Cocktail Bar and Beauty Parlours, its dining-saloons, decorated in more or less credible imitation of the salons of eighteenth-century France, its waiters and guards and attendants of all sorts, its ventilation and heating apparatus as efficient as those of the Strand Palace Hotel, and here we were carrying on as if we were pulling a string of coal trucks.

All the luxury and culture of the world depends ultimately upon the efforts of the labourer. This fact has often been described in books. It has often been the subject of cartoons and pictures—the sweating labourer groaning beneath the weight of all the arts and sciences, the pomps and prides of the world—but here it was in plain daily life.

And what made it even more obvious was the complete absence of connection with the train behind us. The train was there—you could see if it you looked out when going round a bend—but that was all. And just as the passenger very seldom thinks about the men on the engine, so we thought nothing at all about the passengers. They were simply part of the load. Indeed there may not have been any passengers—we weren't aware of any.

And the absence of connection between engine and train was emphasized by the entirely different physical sensations which engine travelling gives you. The noise is different— you never for a moment cease to hear, and to feel, the effort of the pistons. The shriek of the whistle splits your ears, a hundred other noises drown any attempt at conversation.

Though the engine is well sprung, there is a feeling of hard contact on the rails all the time—something like riding on an enormously heavy solid-tyred bicycle. And that rhythmic tune which you hear when travelling in the train, the rhythm of the wheels as they go over the joins in the metals (iddy UMty . . . iddy UMty . . . &c.) is entirely absent. There is simply a continuous iddyiddyiddy . . . there is no sensation of travelling *in* a train—you are travelling *on* an engine. You are on top of an extremely heavy sort of cart-horse which is discharging its terrific pent-up energy by the innumerable outbursts of its breath.

And continuously the fireman works, and continuously the driver, one hand on the throttle lever, the other ready near the brake handle (a handle no bigger than that of a bicycle and yet controlling power sufficient to pull up a train weighing 500 tons) keeps watch on the line ahead for a possible adverse signal. If the signals are down they go straight ahead, slowing down only for the sharper curves and the bigger railway junctions. You place absolute trust in the organization of the line and you know practically every yard of it by sight. You dash roaring into the small black hole of a tunnel (the impression you get is that it's a marvel you don't miss it sometimes) and when you're in you can see nothing at all. Does that make you slow up? Not at all—not by a $\frac{1}{2}$ m.p.h. The signal was down; there *can't* be anything in the way and it's the same at night. I came back on the engine from Grantham in the evening, simply to find out what they *can* see. You can see nothing but the signals—you know your whereabouts simply by memory. And as for the signals: it's surprising how little the green lights show up compared with the red. It seemed to me that they went more by the absence of a red light (in the expected place) than by the presence of a green one. You can see the red miles away but the green only when you're almost on it. And if it seemed a foolhardy proceeding to rush headlong into tunnels in the day time, how much more foolhardy did it seem at night to career along at 80 miles an hour in a black world with nothing to help you but your memory of the road and a lot of flickering lights—lights often almost obliterated by smoke and rain. And here's another primitive thing: You can generally see nothing at all through the glass windows of the cab at night because the reflections of the firelight make it impossible. To see the road, to see the signals, you must put your head out at the side—weather or no. The narrow glass screen prevents your eyes from being filled with smoke and cinders, but, well, it seems a garden of Eden sort of arrangement all the same.

And they don't even fill the tender with coal of the required size. Sometimes a big lump gets wedged into the opening and has to be slowly broken up with a pickaxe before it can be dislodged—what about that? Well, I call it jolly fine; but it's jolly rum too, when you think of all the electric gadgets and labour-saving contrivances which the modern housewife thinks herself a martyr if she don't get.

Up the long bank before Grantham—yes, and you notice the ups and downs when you're on the engine. They are both visible and hearable. You hear the engine's struggle (there's no "changing down" when it starts "labouring"). You feel it too, and looking straight ahead, and not only sideways like the millionaire in the train behind, you see the horizon of the bank before you. It *looks* like a hill. And when you run over the brow you *see* the run down and you hear and feel the engine's change of breath, you hear and feel the more easy thrust of the pistons.

And, on the return journey, going down into London in the dark (on No. 2750 with Mr. Guttridge and Mr. Rayner, a London engine and London men) with steam shut off and fire nearly out—just enough fire to get home with—we were pulled up by an adverse signal. Good that was too. Nothing visible in the blackness but the red lights over our heads. Silence—during which the fireman told me that Mr. Guttridge had driven the King 28 times. Suddenly one of the lights turned green—sort of magical. "Right ho," said the fireman.

ERIC GILL

115. RANNOCH MOOR ON SLEEPERS

I MADE use of the road as long as it kept by the railway that is in the glen leading down to Bridge of Orchy. I then deserted it and turned straight northwards across what looked like a limitless waste of peat and water. My original and foolish intention had been to hold due north and carry on until I reached Rannoch, or saw some house or cottage where I could beg for shelter. I was fortunate enough to be dissuaded from this right at the start by the impossibly boggy ground which I encountered the moment I left the road. I therefore climbed on to the tiny railway embankment and, telling myself that this followed the same course as that which I had proposed to myself, began that dreary business known as "counting the sleepers."

This exercise, which consists of walking along the middle of the railway track and stepping from sleeper to sleeper, is at first very irritating, for no disposition of sleepers ever falls exactly evenly with the length of one's steps. After about a mile or so one gradually begins to alter the natural length of it unconsciously so that it fits the spaces and, if the line has been well laid out and the sleepers do not vary, one swings along with a very easy and regular motion. The eyes are fixed on the track, one hardly notices anything to the right or left of it, and the curves are so gentle as to be unappreciable by the walking traveller. There then begins that half hypnotic effect which is produced by sleeper-counting, and which all who have tramped for any length of time on a railway track have experienced. If one is bored, if one's object is simply to "get there," this drowsiness is pleasant. It can, however, be dangerous if one gets so absorbed as not to notice a train approaching from behind.

The Highland Railway is, I think (for I am quite ignorant of technical matters about gauges), a little narrower than most railways in the United Kingdom. Certainly its sleepers lie a little closer, so it took me some time to get accustomed to the spacing. Moreover, I was continually looking round, stopping, and otherwise distracting my attention from the track in front of me, and was far into the moor before I got anything of a swing into my walk. Even when I did, and was sufficiently bored and tired, I no more lost consciousness of the moor than a meditating fare on a London bus forgets the confusion of the streets through which he travels. It was always beating into my brain, and had so far influenced me that when I stood still and shut my eyes, I could feel that I was standing in an immense space. I could put out my hand and touch the nothingness that pressed in on me.

The Highland Railway, as I have said before, does not rob anything of the grandeur from the scenery through which it passes. It is so insignificant, its trains pass so seldom and so slowly, it no more takes away the desolation from the Highlands for the traveller than does the sight of an Atlantic liner minimize for the swimmer the vastness of the ocean. Roads can much more effectually destroy this quality. The constant stream of different kinds of travellers is continually and regularly interrupting the mind, and is somehow more potent, less laughable than the fussy little train that once every six hours or so snorts its way along the grim track.

On the Moor of Rannoch, even more than in the great mountains, is this harmlessness of the railway noticeable; indeed, it seems in this place to help the really appalling effect of waste around one. The track is a little higher than the land, and if one is walking on it one gets just a slightly longer view over the hillocks and tarns which besprinkle the way. Here and there the track will be banked up and roofed over with corrugated iron so as to prevent, in winter, the drifting snow from holding up the trains; one plunges into these quasi-tunnels almost with relief to escape from the monotony of the scene; and when one emerges at the other end, sometimes a flock of red deer will be startled by this sudden appearance, to skim away like the shadow of a cloud across the ground.

MORAY MCLAREN

116. RANGOON EXPRESS

PUNCTUALLY at 6.15 A.M., to the solemn ringing of handbells, the train steamed out of Mandalay station and headed for the south. Its title, the Rangoon Express, was hardly more than a rhetorical flourish, since among the trains of the world it is probably unique in never reaching its destination. It pushes on, carrying out minor repairs to the track as necessary, unless finally halted by the dynamiting of a bridge. Usually it covers in this way a distance of about 150 miles to reach Yamethin, before turning back. Thereafter follows a sixty-mile stretch along which rarely less than three major bridges are down at any given time, not to mention the absence of eleven miles of permanent way.

Here at Yamethin, then, passengers bound for Rangoon are normally dumped and left to their own ingenuity and fortitude to find their way across the sixty-mile gap to the railhead, at Pyinmana, of the southern section of the line. The last train but one had even ventured past Yamethin, only to be heavily mortared before coming to a final halt at Tatkon; but our immediate predecessor had not done nearly as well, suffering derailment, three days before, at Yeni—about ninety miles south of Mandalay.

Against this background of catastrophe, the Rangoon Express seemed invested with a certain sombre majesty, as it rattled out into the hostile immensity of the plain. Burma was littered with the vestiges of things past: the ten thousand pagodas of vanished kingdoms, and the debris of modern times; smashed stone houses with straw huts built within their walls, and shattered rolling-stock, some already overgrown and some still smelling of charred wood, as we clattered slowly past. In this area, the main towns are held by Government troops, but the country districts are fought over by various insurgent groups—White Flag Communists of the Party line, and their Red Flag deviationist rivals; the P.V.O.s under their *Condottieri*, the Karen Nationalists, and many dacoits. All these battle vigorously with one another, and enter into bewildering series of temporary alliances to fight the Government troops. The result is chaos.

Our train was made up of converted cattle-trucks. Benches, which could be slept on at night, had been fixed up along the length of each compartment. Passengers were recommended to pull the chain in case of emergency, and in the lavatory a notice invited them to depress the handle. But there was no chain and no handle. The electric light came on by twisting two wires together. Protected by the religious scruples of the passengers, giant cockroaches mooched about the floor and clouds of mosquitoes issued from the dark places under the benches. According to the hour, either one side or other of the compartment was scorching hot from the impact of the sun's rays on the outside. This gave passengers sitting on the cooler side the opportunity to demonstrate their good breeding and acquire merit by insisting on changing places with their fellow-travellers sitting opposite.

With the exception of an elderly Buddhist monk, the other occupants of my carriage were railway repairs officials. The monk had recently completed a year of the rigorous penance known as *tapas*, and had just been released from hospital where he had spent six weeks recovering from the effects.

Before taking the yellow robe he too had been a railwayman and could, therefore, enter with vivacity into the technicalities of the others' shop-talk. He had with him a biscuit-tin commemorating the coronation of Edward the Seventh, on which had been screwed a plaque with the inscription in English: "God is Life, Light and Infinite Magnet." From this box he extracted for our entertainment several pre-war copies of *News Digest,* and a collection of snapshots, some depicting railway disasters and others such objects of local veneration as the Buddha-tooth of Kandy.

Delighted to display their inside information of the dangers to which we were exposed, the railway officials kept up a running commentary on the state of the bridges we passed over, all of which had been blown up several times. It was clear that from their familiarity with these hidden structural weaknesses a kind of affection for them had been bred. With relish they disclosed the fact that the supply of new girders had run out, so that the bridges were patched up with doubtfully repaired ones. Similar shortages now compelled them to use two bolts to secure rails to sleepers instead of the regulation four. Smilingly, they sometimes claimed to feel a bridge sway under the train's weight. To illustrate his contention that a driver could easily overlook a small break in the line, a permanent-way inspector mentioned that his "petrol special" had once successfully jumped a gap of twenty inches that no one had noticed. That reminded his friend. The other day his "petrol special" had refused to start after he had been out to inspect a sabotaged bridge, and while he was cleaning the carburettor, a couple of White Flag Communists had come along and taken him to their H.Q. After questioning him about the defences of the local town, they expected him to walk home seven miles through the jungle, although it was after dark. Naturally, he wasn't having any. Insisted on staying the night, and saw to it that they gave him breakfast in the morning. The inspector, who spoke a brand of Asiatic-English current among minor officials, said that they were safe enough going about their work unless accompanied by soldiers. "They observe us at our labours without hindrance. Sometimes a warning shot rings out and we get to hell. That, my dear colleagues, is the set-up. From running continuously I am rejuvenated. All appetites and sleeping much improved."

These pleasant discussions were interrupted in the early afternoon, when a small mine was exploded in front of the engine. A rail had been torn by the explosion, and after allowing the passengers time to marvel at the nearness of their escape, the train began to back towards the station through which we had just passed. Almost immediately, a second mine exploded to the rear of the train, thus immobilising us. The railwaymen seemed surprised at this unusual development. Retiring to the lavatory, the senior inspector reappeared dressed in his best silk *longyi*, determined, it seemed to confront with proper dignity any emergency that might arise. The passengers accepted the situation with the infinite good humour and resignation of the Burmese. We were stranded in a dead-flat sun-wasted landscape. The paddies held a few yellow pools through which black-necked storks waded with premeditation, while buffaloes emerged, as if seen at the moment of creation, from their hidden wallows. About a mile from the line an untidy village broke into the pattern of the fields. You could just make out the point of red where a flag hung from the mogul turret of a house which had once belonged to an Indian landlord. With irrepressible satisfaction the senior inspector said that he knew for certain that there were three hundred Communists in the village. Going by past experience, he did not expect that they would attack the train, but a squad might be sent to look over the passengers. When I asked whether they would be likely to take away any European they found, the old monk said that they would not dare to do so in the face of his prohibition. He added that Buddhist monks preached and collected their rice in Communist villages without interference from party officials. This, he believed, was due to the fact that the Buddhist priesthood had never sided with oppressors. Their complete neutrality being recognised by all sides, they were also often asked both by the Government and the various insurgent groups to act as intermediaries.

And, in fact, there was no sign of life from the village. Time passed slowly and the monk entertained the company, discoursing with priestly erudition on such topics as the history of the great King Mindon's previous incarnation as a female demon. A Deputy Inspector of Waggons, who was also a photographic enthusiast, described a camera he had seen with which subjects, when photographed in normal attire, came out in the nude. The misfortunes of the Government were discussed with much speculation as to their cause, and there was some support for a rumour, widespread in Burma, that this was ascribable to the incompetence of the astrologer who had calculated the propitious hour and day for the declaration of Independence.

With much foresight, spare rails were carried on the train and, some hours later, a "petrol special" arrived with a breakdown gang. It also brought vendors of *samusa* (mincemeat and onion patties in puff pastry), fried chicken, and Vimtonic —a non-alcoholic beverage in great local demand. Piously, the Buddhist monk restricted himself to rice, baked in the hollow of a yard-long cane of bamboo, subsequently sucking a couple of mepachrine tablets, under the impression that they contained vitamins valuable to his weakened state.

Quite soon the damaged rail ahead had been replaced, and we were on our way again, reaching, soon after nightfall, the town of Yamethin. Yamethin is known as the hottest town in Burma. It was waterless, but you could buy a slab of ice-cream on a stick, and the Chinese proprietor of the tea-shop made no charge for plain tea if you bought a cake. With traditional magnificence a burgher of the town had chosen to celebrate some windfall by offering his fellow citizens a free theatrical show, which was being performed in the station yard. It was a well-loved piece dealing with a profligate queen of old, who had remarkably chosen to cuckold the king with a legless dwarf. The show was to last all night, and at one moment, between the squealing and the banging of the orchestra, could be heard the thump of bombs falling in a nearby village.

It was only here and now that the real problem of the day arose. Since we were to sleep in the train, who was to occupy the upper berths, now fixed invitingly in position? Whoever did so would thus be compelled to show disrespect to those sleeping beneath them; a situation intolerably aggravated in this case by the presence of the venerable monk who was in no state to climb to the higher position. Of such things were composed, for a Burman, the true hardships of travel in troublous lines. The perils and discomforts attendant upon the collapse of law and order were of no ultimate consequence. What was really important was the unswerving correctness of one's deportment in facing them.

NORMAN LEWIS

II. FANCY

117. THROUGH THE LOOKING GLASS

"Tickets, please!" said the Guard, putting his head in at the window. In a moment everybody was holding out a ticket: they were about the same size as the people, and quite seemed to fill the carriage.

"Now then! Show your ticket, child!" the Guard went on, looking angrily at Alice. And a great many voices all said together ("like the chorus of a song," thought Alice), "Don't keep him waiting, child! Why, his time is worth a thousand pounds a minute!"

"I'm afraid I haven't got one," Alice said in a frightened tone: "there wasn't a ticket-office where I came from." And again the chorus of voices went on. "There wasn't room for one where she came from. The land there is worth a thousand pounds an inch!"

"Don't make excuses," said the Guard: "you should have bought one from the engine-driver." And once more the chorus of voices went on with "The man that drives the engine. Why, the smoke alone is worth a thousand pounds a puff!"

Alice thought to herself, "Then there's no use in speaking." The voices didn't join in this time, as she hadn't spoken, but, to her great surprise, they all *thought* in chorus (I hope you understand what *thinking in chorus* means—for I must confess *I* don't), "Better say nothing at all. Language is worth a thousand pounds a word!"

"I shall dream about a thousand pounds to-night, I know I shall!" thought Alice.

All this time the Guard was looking at her, first through a

telescope, then through a microscope, and then through an opera-glass. At last he said "You're travelling the wrong way," and shut up the window and went away.

"So young a child," said the gentleman sitting opposite to her, (he was dressed in white paper,) "ought to know which way she's going, even if she doesn't know her own name!"

A Goat, that was sitting next to the gentleman in white, shut his eyes and said in a loud voice, "She ought to know her way to the ticket-office, even if she doesn't know her alphabet!"

There was a Beetle sitting next the Goat (it was a very queer carriage full of passengers altogether), and as the rule seemed to be that they should all speak in turn, *he* went on with "She'll have to go back from here as luggage!"

Alice couldn't see who was sitting beyond the Beetle, but a hoarse voice spoke next. "Change engines———" it said, and there it choked and was obliged to leave off.

"It sounds like a horse," Alice thought to herself. And an extremely small voice, close to her ear, said "You might make a joke on that—something about 'horse' and 'hoarse', you know."

Then a very gentle voice in the distance said, "She must be labelled 'Lass with care,' you know———"

And after that other voices went on ("What a number of people there are in the carriage!" thought Alice), saying "She must go by post, as she's got a head on her———" "She must be sent as a message by the telegraph———" "She must draw the train herself the rest of the way———", and so on.

But the gentleman dressed in white paper leaned forwards and whispered in her ear, "Never mind what they all say, my dear, but take a return-ticket every time the train stops."

"Indeed I sha'n't!" Alice said rather impatiently. "I don't belong to this railway journey at all—I was in a wood just now—and I wish I could get back there."

"You might make a joke on *that*," said the little voice close to her ear: "something about you *would* if you could, you know."

"Don't tease so," said Alice looking about in vain to see where the voice came from; "if you're so anxious to have a joke made, why don't you make one yourself?"

The little voice sighed deeply: it was *very* unhappy evidently, and Alice would have said something pitying to comfort it, "if it would only sigh like other people!" she thought. But this was such a wonderfully small sigh, that she wouldn't have heard it at all, if it hadn't come *quite* close to her ear. The consequence of this was that it tickled her ear very much, and quite took off her thoughts from the unhappiness of the poor little creature.

"I know you are a friend," the little voice went on; "a dear friend, and an old friend. And you won't hurt me though I *am* an insect."

"What kind of insect?" Alice inquired a little anxiously. What she really wanted to know was, whether it could sting or not, but she thought this wouldn't be quite a civil question to ask.

"What, then you don't——" the little voice began, when it was drowned by a shrill scream from the engine, and everybody jumped up in alarm, Alice among the rest.

The Horse, who had put his head out of the window, quietly drew it in and said "It's only a brook we have to jump over." Everybody seemed satisfied with this, though Alice felt a little nervous at the idea of trains jumping at all. "However, it will take us into the Fourth Square, that's some comfort!" she said to herself. In another moment she felt the carriage rise straight up into the air, and in her fright she caught at the thing nearest to her hand, which happened to be the Goat's beard.

LEWIS CARROLL

118. MIDNIGHT ON THE GREAT WESTERN

In the third-class seat sat the journeying boy,
    And the roof-lamp's oily flame
Played down on his listless form and face,
Bewrapt past knowing to what he was going,
    Or whence he came.

In the band of his hat the journeying boy
    Had a ticket stuck; and a string
Around his neck bore the key of his box,
That twinkled gleams of the lamp's sad beams
    Like a living thing.

What past can be yours, O journeying boy
    Towards a world unknown,
Who calmly, as if incurious quite
To all at stake, can undertake
    This plunge alone?

Knows your soul a sphere, O journeying boy,
    Our rude realms far above,
Whence with spacious vision you mark and mete
This region of sin that you find you in,
    But are not of?

THOMAS HARDY

119. THE NIGHT JOURNEY

Hand and lit faces eddy to a line;
    The dazed last minutes click; the clamour dies.
Beyond the great-swung arc o' the roof, divine,
    Night, smoky-scarv'd, with thousand coloured eyes

Glares the imperious mystery of the way.
  Thirsty for dark, you feel the long-limbed train
Throb, stretch, thrill motion, slide, pull out and sway,
  Strain for the far, pause, draw to strength again . . .

As a man, caught by some great hour, will rise,
  Slow-limbed, to meet the light or find his love;
And, breathing long, with staring, sightless eyes,
  Hands out, head back, agape and silent, move

Sure as a flood, smooth as a vast wind blowing;
  And, gathering power and purpose as he goes,
Unstumbling, unreluctant, strong, unknowing,
  Borne by a will not his, that lifts, that grows,

Sweep out to darkness, triumphing in his goal,
  Out of the fire, out of the little room. . . .
—There is an end appointed, O my soul!
  Crimson and green the signals burn; the gloom

Is hung with steam's far-blowing livid streamers.
  Lost into God, as lights in light, we fly,
Grown one with will, end-drunken huddled dreamers.
  The white lights roar. The sounds of the world die.

And lips and laughter are forgotten things.
  Speed sharpens; grows. Into the night, and on,
The strength and splendour of our purpose swings.
  The lamps fade; and the stars. We are alone.

RUPERT BROOKE

120. THE MONOMANIAC

AT last, Pecqueux with a final spurt, precipitated Jacques from the engine; but the latter, feeling himself in space, clung so tightly in his bewilderment to the neck of his antagonist, that he dragged Pecqueux along with him. There were a couple of terrible shrieks, which mingled one with the other and were lost. The two men falling together, cast under the wheels by the counter-shock, were cut to pieces clasping one another in that frightful embrace—they, who so long had lived as brothers. They were found without heads, and without feet, two bleeding trunks, still hugging as if to choke each other.

And the engine, free from all guidance rolled on and on. At last the restive, whimsical thing could give way to the transports of youth, and gallop across the even country like some unbroken filly escaped from the hands of its groom. The boiler was full of water, the coal which had just been renewed in the fire-box, was aglow; and during the last half-hour the pressure went up tremendously, while the speed became frightful. Probably the headguard, overcome with fatigue, had fallen asleep. The soldiers, whose intoxication increased through being packed so closely together, suddenly became amused at this rapid flight of the train, and sang the louder. Maromme was passed in a flash. The whistle no longer sounded as the signals were approached, and the stations reached. This was the straight gallop of an animal charging, head down and silent, amidst the obstacles. And it rolled on and on without end, as if maddened more and more by the strident sound of its breath.

At Rouen the engine should have taken in water; and the people at the station were struck with terror when they saw this mad train dart by in a whirl of smoke and flame; the locomotive without driver or fireman, the cattle-trucks full of soldiers yelling patriotic songs. They were going to the war, and if the train did not stop it was in order that they might arrive more rapidly yonder, on the banks of the Rhine. The railway servants stood gaping, agitating their arms. Immediately there was one general cry, this train let loose, abandoned to itself, would never pass without impediment through Sotteville station, which was always blocked by shunting manœuvres and obstructed by carriages and engines like all great depôts. And there was a rush to the telegraph-office to give warning.

At Sotteville a goods train, occupying the line, was shunted just in time. Already the rumble of the escaped monster could be heard in the distance. It had dashed into the two tunnels in the vicinity of Rouen, and was arriving at its furious gallop like a prodigious and irresistible force that naught could now stay; and Sotteville station was left behind. It passed among the obstacles without touching anything, and again plunged into the obscurity where its roar gradually died away.

But now, all the telegraphic apparatus on the line was tinkling, all hearts were beating at the news of the phantom train which had just been seen passing through Rouen and Sotteville. Everyone trembled with fear, an express on ahead would certainly be caught up. The runaway, like a wild boar in the underwood, continued its course without giving any attention either to red lights or crackers. It almost ran into a pilot-engine at Oissel and terrified Pont-de-l'Arche, for its speed showed no signs of slackening. Again it had disappeared, and it rolled on and on in the obscure night, going none knew where—yonder.

What mattered the victims the engine crushed on the road! Was it not advancing towards the future in spite of all, heedless of the blood that might be spilt? Without a guide, amidst the darkness, like an animal blind and dumb let loose

amidst death, it rolled on and on, loaded with this food for
cannon, with these soldiers already besotted with fatigue and
drink, who were singing.

ÉMILE ZOLA

121. DYKE'S LAST DRIVE

WEEKS of flight had sharpened Dyke's every sense. As he
turned into the Upper Road beyond Guadalajara, he saw the
three men galloping down from Derrick's stock range,
making for the road ahead of him. They would cut him off
there. He swung the buckskin about. He must take the
Lower Road across Los Muertos from Guadalajara, and he
must reach it before Delaney's dogs and posse. Back he
galloped, the buckskin measuring her length with every leap.
Once more the station came in sight. Rising in his stirrups
he looked across the fields in the direction of the Lower Road.
There was a cloud of dust there. From a wagon? No, horses
on the run, and their riders were armed! He could catch the
flash of gun barrels. They were all closing in on him, con-
verging on Guadalajara by every available road. The Upper
Road west of Guadalajara led straight to Bonneville. That
way was impossible. Was he in a trap? Had the time for
fighting come at last?

But as Dyke neared the depot at Guadalajara, his eye fell
upon the detached locomotive that lay quietly steaming on
the up line, and with a thrill of exultation, he remembered
that he was an engineer born and bred. Delaney's dogs were
already to be heard, and the roll of hoofs on the Lower Road
was dinning in his ears, as he leaped from the buckskin
before the depot. The train crew scattered like frightened
sheep before him, but Dyke ignored them. His pistol was in
his hand as, once more on foot, he sprang toward the lone
engine.

"Out of the cab," he shouted. "Both of you. Quick, or I'll kill you both."

The two men tumbled from the iron apron of the tender as Dyke swung himself up, dropping his pistol on the floor of the cab and reaching with the old instinct for the familiar levers.

The great compound hissed and trembled as the steam was released, and the huge drivers stirred, turning slowly on the tracks. But there was a shout. Delaney's posse, dogs and men, swung into view at the end of the road, their figures leaning over as they took the curve at full speed. Dyke threw everything wide open and caught up his revolver. From behind came the challenge of a Winchester. The party on the Lower Road were even closer than Delaney. They had seen his manœuvre, and the first shot of the fight shivered the cab windows above the engineer's head.

But spinning futilely at first, the drivers of the engine at last caught the rails. The engine moved, advanced, travelled past the depot and the freight train, and gathering speed, rolled out on the track beyond. Smoke, black and boiling, shot skyward from the stack; not a joint that did not shudder with the mighty strain of the steam; but the great iron brute —one of Baldwin's newest and best—came to call, obedient and docile as soon as ever the great pulsing heart of it felt a master hand upon its levers. It gathered its speed, bracing its steel muscles, its thews of iron, and roared out upon the open track, filling the air with the raps of its tempest-breath, blotting the sunshine with the belch of its hot, thick smoke. Already it was lessening in the distance, when Delaney, Christian, and the sheriff of Visalia dashed up to the station.

The posse had seen everything.

"Stuck. Curse the luck!" vociferated the cow-puncher.

But the sheriff was already out of the saddle and into the telegraph office.

"There's a derailing switch between here and Pixley, isn't there?" he cried.

"Yes."

"Wire ahead to open it. We'll derail him there. Come on"; he turned to Delaney and the others. They sprang into the cab of the locomotive that was attached to the freight train.

"Name of the State of California," shouted the sheriff to the bewildered engineer. "Cut off from your train."

The sheriff was a man to be obeyed without hesitating. Time was not allowed the crew of the freight train for debating as to the right or wrong of requisitioning the engine, and before anyone thought of the safety or danger of the affair, the freight engine was already flying out upon the down line, hot in pursuit of Dyke, now far ahead upon the up track.

"I remember perfectly there's a derailing switch between here and Pixley," shouted the sheriff above the roar of the locomotive. "They use it in case they have to derail runaway engines. It runs right off into the country. We'll pile him up there. Ready with your guns, boys."

"If we should meet another train coming up on this track—" protested the frightened engineer.

"Then we'd jump or be smashed. Hi! look! There he is." As the freight engine rounded a curve, Dyke's engine came into view, shooting on some quarter of a mile ahead of them, wreathed in whirling smoke.

"The switch ain't much further on," clamoured the engineer. "You can see Pixley now."

Dyke, his hand on the grip of the valve that controlled the steam, his head out of the cab window, thundered on. He was back in his old place again; once more he was the engineer; once more he felt the engine quiver under him; the familiar noises were in his ears; the familiar buffeting of the wind surged, roaring at his face; the familiar odour of hot steam and smoke reeked in his nostrils, and on either side of him, parallel panoramas, the two halves of the landscape sliced, as it were, in two by the clashing wheels of his engine, streamed by in green and brown blurs.

He found himself settling to the old position on the cab seat, leaning on his elbow from the window, one hand on the controller. All at once, the instinct of the pursuit that of late had become so strong in him, prompted him to shoot a glance behind. He saw the other engine on the down line, plunging after him, rocking from side to side with the fury of its gallop. Not yet had he shaken the trackers from his heels; not yet was he out of the reach of danger. He set his teeth and, throwing open the fire-door, stoked vigorously for a few moments. The indicator of the steam gauge rose; his speed increased; a glance at the telegraph poles told him he was doing his fifty miles an hour. The freight engine behind him was never built for that pace. Barring the terrible risk of an accident, his chances were good.

But suddenly—the engineer dominating the highwayman —he shut off steam and threw back his brake to the extreme notch. Directly ahead of him rose a semaphore, placed at a point where evidently a derailing switch branched from the line. The semaphore's arm was dropped over the track, setting the danger signal that showed the switch was open.

In an instant, Dyke saw the trick. They had meant to smash him here; had been clever enough, quick-witted enough, to open the switch, but had forgotten the automatic semaphore that worked simultaneously with the movement of the rails. To go forward was certain destruction. Dyke reversed. There was nothing for it but to go back. With a wrench and a spasm of all its metal fibres, the great compound braced itself, sliding with rigid wheels along the rails. Then, as Dyke applied the reverse, it drew back from the greater danger, returning towards the less. Inevitably now the two engines, one on the up, the other on the down line, must meet and pass each other.

Dyke released the levers, reaching for his revolver. The engineer once more became the highwayman, in peril of his life. Now, beyond all doubt, the time for fighting was at hand.

The party in the heavy freight engine, that lumbered after in pursuit, their eyes fixed on the smudge of smoke on ahead that marked the path of the fugitive, suddenly raised a shout. "He's stopped. He's broke down. Watch, now, and see if he jumps off."

"Broke *nothing. He's coming back.* Ready, now, he's got to pass us."

The engineer applied the brakes, but the heavy freight locomotive, far less mobile than Dyke's flyer, was slow to obey. The smudge on the rails ahead grew swiftly larger.

"He's coming. He's coming—look out, there's a shot. He's shooting already."

A bright, white sliver of wood leaped into the air from the sooty window sill of the cab.

"Fire on him! Fire on him!"

While the engines were yet two hundred yards apart, the duel began, shot answering shot, the sharp staccato reports punctuating the thunder of wheels and the clamour of steam.

Then the ground trembled and rocked; a roar as of heavy ordnance developed with the abruptness of an explosion. The two engines passed each other, the men firing the while, emptying their revolvers, shattering wood, shivering glass, the bullets clanging against the metal work as they struck and struck and struck. The men leaned from the cabs towards each other, frantic with excitement, shouting curses, the engines rocking, the steam roaring; confusion whirling in the scene like the whirl of a witch's dance, the white clouds of steam, the black eddies from the smokestack, the blue wreaths from the hot mouths of revolvers, swirling together in a blinding maze of vapour, spinning around them, dazing them, dizzying them, while the head rang with hideous clamour and the body twitched and trembled with the leap and jar of the tumult of machinery.

Roaring, clamouring, reeking with the smell of powder and hot oil, spitting death, resistless, huge, furious, an abrupt vision of chaos, faces, rage-distorted, peering through smoke, hands gripping outward from sudden darkness, prehensile, malevolent; terrible as thunder, swift as lightning, the two engines met and passed.

"He's hit," cried Delaney. "I know I hit him. He can't go far now. After him again. He won't dare go through Bonneville."

It was true. Dyke had stood between cab and tender throughout all the duel, exposed, reckless, thinking only of attack and not of defence, and a bullet from one of the pistols had grazed his hip. How serious was the wound he did not know, but he had no thought of giving up. He tore back through the depot at Guadalajara in a storm of bullets, and, clinging to the broken window ledge of his cab, was carried towards Bonneville, on over the Long Trestle and Broderson Creek and through the open country between the two ranches of Los Muertos and Quien Sabe.

But to go on to Bonneville meant certain death. Before, as well as behind him, the roads were now blocked. Once more he thought of the mountains. He resolved to abandon the engine and make another final attempt to get into the shelter of the hills in the northernmost corner of Quien Sabe. He set his teeth. He would not give in. There was one more fight left in him yet. Now to try the final hope.

He slowed the engine down, and, reloading his revolver, jumped from the platform to the road. He looked about him, listening. All around him widened an ocean of wheat. There was no one in sight.

The released engine, alone, unattended, drew slowly away from him, jolting ponderously over the rail joints. As he watched it go, a certain indefinite sense of abandonment, even in that moment, came over Dyke. His last friend, that also had been his first, was leaving him. He remembered that day, long ago, when he had opened the throttle of his first machine. To-day, it was leaving him alone, his last friend turning against him. Slowly it was going back towards Bonneville, to the shops of the Railroad, the camp of the enemy, that enemy that had ruined him and wrecked him. For the last time in his life, he had been the engineer. Now, once more, he became the highwayman, the outlaw against whom all hands were raised, the fugitive skulking in the mountains, listening for the cry of dogs.

FRANK NORRIS

122. BEATTOCK FOR MOFFAT

The bustle on the Euston platform stopped for an instant to let the men who carried him to the third-class compartment pass along the train. Gaunt and emaciated, he looked just at death's door, and, as they propped him in the carriage between two pillows, he faintly said, "Jock, do ye think I'll live as far as Moffat? I should na' like to die in London in the smoke."

His cockney wife, drying her tears with a cheap hem-stitched pocket handkerchief, her scanty town-bred hair looking like wisps of tow beneath her hat, bought from some window in which each individual article was marked at seven-and-sixpence, could only sob. His brother, with the country sun and wind burn still upon his face, and his huge hands hanging like hams in front of him, made answer.

"Andra'," he said, "gin ye last as far as Beattock, we'll gie ye a braw hurl back to the farm, syne the bask air, ye ken, and the milk, and, and—but can ye last as far as Beattock, Andra'?"

The sick man, sitting with the cold sweat upon his face, his shrunken limbs looking like sticks inside his ill-made black slop suit, after considering the proposition on its merits, looked up, and said, "I should na' like to bet I feel fair boss, God knows; but there, the mischief of it is, he will na' tell ye, so that, as ye may say, his knowlidge has na' commercial value. I ken I look as gash as Garscadden. Ye mind, Jock, in the braw auld times, when the auld laird just slipped away, whiles they were birlin' at the clairet. A braw death, Jock . . . do ye think it'll be rainin' aboot Ecclefechan? Aye . . . sure to be rainin' aboot Lockerbie. Nae Christians there, Jock, a' Johnstones and Jardines, ye mind?"

The wife, who had been occupied with an air cushion, and, having lost the bellows, had been blowing into it till her cheeks seemed almost bursting, and her false teeth were loosened in her head, left off her toil to ask her husband "If 'e could pick a bit of something, a porkpie, or a nice sausage roll, or something tasty," which she could fetch from the refreshment room. The invalid having declined to eat, and his brother having drawn from his pocket a dirty bag, in which were peppermints, gave him a "drop," telling him that he "minded he aye used to like them weel, when the meenister had fairly got into his prelection in the auld kirk, outby."

The train slid almost imperceptibly away, the passengers upon the platform looking after it with that half foolish, half astonished look with which men watch a disappearing train. Then a few sandwich papers rose with the dust almost to the level of the platform, sank again, the clock struck twelve and the station fell into a half quiescence, like a volcano in the interval between the lava showers. Inside the third-class carriage all was quiet until the lights of Harrow shone upon the

left, when the sick man, turning himself with difficulty, said,
"Good-bye, Harrow-on-the-Hill. I aye liked Harrow for
the hill's sake, tho' ye can scarcely ca' yon wee bit mound a
hill, Jean."

His wife, who, even in her grief, still smarted under the
Scotch variant of her name, which all her life she had pronounced as "Jayne," and who, true cockney as she was,
bounded her world within the lines of Plaistow, Peckham
Rye, the Welsh 'Arp ('Endon way), and Willesden, moved
uncomfortably at the depreciation of the chief mountain in
her cosmos, but held her peace. Loving her husband in a
sort of half-antagonistic fashion, born of the difference of
type between the hard, unyielding, yet humorous and sentimental Lowland Scot, and the conglomerate of all races of
the island which meet in London, and produce the weedy,
shallow breed, almost incapable of reproduction, and yet
high-strung and nervous, there had arisen between them that
intangible veil of misconception which, though not excluding
love, is yet impervious to respect. Each saw the other's fail-
ings, or, perhaps, thought the good qualities which each
possessed were faults, for usually men judge each other by
their good points, which, seen through prejudice of race,
religion, and surroundings, appear to them defects.

The brother, who but a week ago had left his farm unwil-
lingly, just when the "neeps were wantin' heughin' and a feck
o' things requirin' to be done, forby a puckle sheep waitin'
for keelin'," to come and see his brother for the last time, sat
in that dour and seeming apathetic attitude which falls upon
the country man, torn from his daily toil, and plunged into a
town. Most things in London, during the brief intervals he
had passed away from the sick-bed, seemed foolish to him,
and of a nature such as a self-respecting Moffat man, in the
hebdomadal enjoyment of the "prelections" of a Free Church
minister, could not authorise.

"Man, saw ye e'er a carter sittin' on his cart, and drivin' at a trot, instead o' walkin' in a proper manner alongside his horse?" had been his first remark.

The short-tailed sheep-dogs, and the way they worked, the inferior quality of the carthorses, their shoes with hardly any calkins worth the name, all was repugnant to him.

On Sabbath, too, he had received a shock, for, after walking miles to sit under the "brither of the U.P. minister at Symington," he had found Erastian hymn books in the pews, and noticed with stern reprobation that the congregation stood to sing and that, instead of sitting solidly whilst the "man wrastled in prayer," stooped forward in the fashion called the Nonconformist lounge.

His troubled spirit had received refreshment from the sermon, which, though short, and extending to but some five-and-forty minutes, had still been powerful, for he said:

"When yon wee, shilpit meenister—brither, ye ken, of rantin' Ferguson, out by Symington—shook the congregation ower the pit mouth, ye could hae fancied that the very sowls in hell just girned. Man, he garred the very stour to flee aboot the kirk, and, hadna' the big book been weel brass banded, he would hae dang the haricles fair oot."

So the train slipped past Watford, swaying round the curves like a gigantic serpent, and jolting at the facing points as a horse "pecks" in his gallop at an obstruction in the ground.

The moon shone brightly into the compartment, extinguishing the flickering of the half-candle-power electric light. Rugby, the station all lit up, and with its platforms occupied but by a few belated passengers, all muffled up like racehorses taking their exercise, flashed past. They slipped through Cannock Chase, which stretches down with heath and firs, clear brawling streams, and birch trees, an out-post of the north lost in the midland clay. They crossed the oily

Trent, flowing through alder copses, and with its backwaters all overgrown with lilies, like an "aguapey" in Paraguay or in Brazil.

The sick man, wrapped in cheap rugs, and sitting like Guy Fawkes, in the half comic, half pathetic way that sick folk sit, making them sport for fools, and, at the same time, moistening the eye of the judicious, who reflect that they themselves may one day sit as they do, bereft of all the dignity of strength, looked listlessly at nothing as the train sped on. His loving, tactless wife, whose cheap "sized" handkerchief had long since become a rag with mopping up her tears, endeavoured to bring round her husband's thoughts to paradise, which she conceived a sort of music hall, where angels sat with their wings folded, listening to sentimental songs.

Her brother-in-law, reared on the fiery faith of Moffat Calvinism, eyed her with great disfavour, as a terrier eyes a rat imprisoned in a cage.

"Jean wumman," he burst out, "to hear ye talk, I would jist think your meenister had been a perfectly illeeterate man, pairadise here, pairadise there, what do ye think a man like Andra could dae daunderin' aboot a gairden naked, pu'in soor aipples frae the trees?"

Cockney and Scotch conceit, impervious alike to outside criticism, and each so bolstered in its pride as to be quite incapable of seeing that anything existed outside the purlieus of their sight, would soon have made the carriage into a battle-field, had not the husband, with the authority of approaching death, put in his word.

"Whist, Jeanie wumman. Jock, dae ye no ken that the Odium-Theologicum is just a curse—pairadise—set ye baith up—pairadise. I dinna' even richtly ken if I can last as far as Beattock."

Stafford, its iron furnaces belching out flames, which burned red holes into the night, seemed to approach, rather

than be approached, so smoothly ran the train. The mingled
moonlight and the glare of iron-works lit the canal beside the
railway, and from the water rose white vapours as from Styx
or Periphlegethon. Through Cheshire ran the train, its
timbered houses showing ghastly in the frost which coated all
the carriage windows, and rendered them opaque. Preston,
the catholic city, lay silent in the night, its river babbling
through the public park, and then the hills of Lancashire
loomed lofty in the night. Past Garstang, with its water-
lily-covered ponds, Garstang where, in the days gone by,
catholic squires, against their will, were forced on Sundays to
"take wine" in Church on pain of fine, the puffing serpent slid.

The talk inside the carriage had given place to sleep, that
is, the brother-in-law and wife slept fitfully, but the sick man
looked out, counting the miles to Moffat, and speculating on
his strength. Big drops of sweat stood on his forehead, and
his breath came double, whistling through his lungs.

They passed by Lancaster, skirting the sea on which the
moon shone bright, setting the fishing boats in silver as they
lay scarcely moving on the waves. Then, so to speak, the
train set its face up against Shap Fell, and, puffing heavily,
drew up into the hills, the scattered grey stone houses of the
north, flanked by their gnarled and twisted ash trees, hanging upon the edge of the streams, as lonely, and as cut off
from the world (except the passing train) as they had been in
Central Africa. The moorland roads, winding amongst the
heather, showed that the feet of generations had marked them
out, and not the line, spade, and theodolite, with all the
circumstance of modern road makers. They, too, looked
white and unearthly in the moonlight, and now and then a
sheep, aroused by the snorting of the train, moved from the
heather into the middle of the road, and stood there motionless, its shadow filling the narrow track, and flickering on the
heather at the edge.

The keen and penetrating air of the hills and night aroused the two sleepers, and they began to talk, after the Scottish fashion, of the funeral, before the anticipated corpse.

"Ye ken, we've got a braw new hearse outby, sort of Epescopalian-lookin', we' gless a' roond, so's ye can see the kist. Very conceity too, they mak' the hearses noo-a-days. I min' when they were jist auld sort o' ruckly boxes, awfu' licht, ye ken, upon the springs, and just went dodderin' alang, the body swingin' to and fro, as if it would flee richt oot. The roads, ye ken, were no high hand so richtly metalled in thae days."

The subject of the conversation took it cheerfully, expressing pleasure at the advance of progress as typified in the new hearse, hoping his brother had a decent "stan' o' black," and looking at his death, after the fashion of his kind, as it were something outside himself, a fact indeed, on which, at the same time, he could express himself with confidence as being in some measure interested. His wife, not being Scotch, took quite another view, and seemed to think that the mere mention of the word was impious, or, at the least, of such a nature as to bring on immediate dissolution, holding the English theory that unpleasant things should not be mentioned, and that, by this means, they can be kept at bay. Half from affection, half from the inborn love of cant, inseparable from the true Anglo-Saxon, she endeavoured to persuade her husband that he looked better, and yet would mend, once in his native air.

"At Moffit, ye'd 'ave the benefit of the 'ill breezes, and that 'ere country milk, which never 'as no cream in it, but 'ole-some, as you say. Why yuss, in about eight days at Moffit, you'll be as 'earty as you ever was. Yuss, you will, you take my word."

Like a true Londoner, she did not talk religion, being too thin in mind and body even to have grasped the dogma of the sects. Her Heaven a music 'all, her paradise to see the king drive through the streets, her literary pleasure to read lies in newspapers, or pore on novelettes, which showed her the pure elevated lives of duchesses, placing the knaves and prostitutes within the limits of her own class; which view of life she accepted as quite natural, and as a thing ordained to be by the bright stars who write.

Just at the Summit they stopped an instant to let a goods train pass, and, in a faint voice, the consumptive said, "I'd almost lay a wager now I'd last to Moffat, Jock. The Shap, ye ken, I aye looked at as the beginning of the run home. The hills, ye ken, are sort o' heartsome. No that they're bonny hills like Moffat hills, na', na', ill-shapen sort of things, just like Borunty tatties, awfu' puir names too, Shap Fell and Rowland Edge, Hutton Roof Crags, and Arnside Fell; heard ever ony body sich like names for hills? Naething to fill the mooth; man, the Scotch hills jist grap ye in the mooth for a' the world like speerits."

They stopped at Penrith, which the old castle walls make even meaner, in the cold morning light, than other stations look. Little Salkeld, and Armathwaite, Cotehill, and Scotby all rushed past, and the train, slackening, stopped with a jerk upon the platform, at Carlisle. The sleepy porters bawled out "change for Maryport," some drovers slouched into carriages, kicking their dogs before them, and, slamming-to the doors, exchanged the time of day with others of their tribe, all carrying ash or hazel sticks, all red-faced and keen-eyed, their caps all crumpled, and their greatcoat tails all creased, as if their wearers had laid down to sleep full dressed, so as to lose no time in getting to the labours of the day. The old red sandstone church, with something of a castle in its look, as well befits a shrine close to a frontier where in days gone by the priest had need to watch and pray, frowned on the passing train, and on the manufactories, whose banked-up fires sent poisonous fumes into the air, withering the trees, which, in the public park, a careful council had hedged round about with wire.

The Eden ran from bank to bank, its water swirling past as wildly as when "The Bauld Buccleugh" and his Moss Troopers, bearing "the Kinmount" fettered in their midst, plunged in and passed it, whilst the keen Lord Scroope stood on the brink amazed and motionless. Gretna, so close to England, and yet a thousand miles away in speech and feeling, found the sands now flying through the glass. All through the mosses which once were the "Debateable Land" on which the moss-troopers of the clan Graeme were used to hide the cattle stolen from the "auncient enemy," the now repatriated Scotchman murmured feebly "that it was bonny scenery" although a drearier prospect of "moss hags" and stunted birch trees is not to be found. At Ecclefechan he just raised his head, and faintly spoke of "yon auld carle, Carlyle, ye ken, a dour thrawn body, but a gran' pheelosopher," and then lapsed into silence, broken by frequent struggles to take breath.

His wife and brother sat still, and eyed him as a cow watches a locomotive engine pass, amazed and helpless, and he himself had but the strength to whisper "Jock, I'm dune, I'll no' see Moffat, blast it, yon smoke, ye ken, yon London smoke has been ower muckle for ma lungs."

The tearful, helpless wife, not able even to pump up the harmful and unnecessary conventional lie, which after all, consoles only the liar, sat pale and limp, chewing the fingers of her Berlin gloves. Upon the weather-beaten cheek of Jock glistened a tear, which he brushed off as angrily as it had been a wasp.

"Aye, Andra'," he said, "I would hae liket awfu' weel that ye should win to Moffat. Man, the rowan trees are a' in bloom, and there's a bonny breer upon the corn—aye, ou

aye, the reid bogs are lookin' gran' the year—but Andra',
I'll tak' ye east to the auld kirk yaird, ye'll no' ken onything
aboot it, but we'll hae a heartsome funeral."

Lockerbie seemed to fly towards them, and the dying
Andra' smiled as his brother pointed out the place and said,
"Ye mind, there are no ony Christians in it," and answered,
"Aye, I mind naething but Jardines," as he fought for breath.

The death dews gathered on his forehead as the train shot
by Nethercleugh, passed Wamphray, and Dinwoodie, and
with a jerk pulled up at Beattock just at the summit of the
pass.

So in the cold spring morning light, the fine rain beating
on the platform, as the wife and brother got their almost
speechless care out of the carriage, the brother whispered,
"Dam't, ye've done it, Andra', here's Beattock; I'll tak' ye
east to Moffat yet to dee."

But on the platform, huddled on the bench to which he
had been brought, Andra' sat speechless and dying in the
rain. The doors banged to, the guard stepping in lightly as
the train flew past, and a belated porter shouted, "Beattock,
Beattock for Moffat," and then, summoning his last strength,
Andra' smiled, and whispered faintly in his brother's ear,
"Aye, Beattock—for Moffat?" Then his head fell back, and
a faint bloody foam oozed from his pallid lips. His wife
stood crying helplessly, the rain beating upon the flowers of
her cheap hat, rendering it shapeless and ridiculous. But Jock,
drawing out a bottle, took a short dram and saying, "Andra',
man, ye made a richt gude fecht o' it," snorted an instant in
a red pocket handkerchief, and calling up a boy, said, "Rin,
Jamie, to the toon, and tell McNicol to send up and fetch a
corp." Then, after helping to remove the body to the
waiting-room, walked out into the rain, and, whistling "Corn
Rigs" quietly between his teeth lit up his pipe, and muttered
as he smoked "A richt gude fecht—man aye, ou aye, a game

yin Andra', puir felly. Weel, weel, he'll hae a braw hurl
onyway in the new Moffat hearse."

R. B. CUNNINGHAME GRAHAM

123. THE BUG

THEY encountered it after an indefinite wait at a junction
during which they were subjected to a somewhat perfunctory
Customs examination, and when it finally appeared it looked
less like a train of any description than a stunted single-decker
bus—or it would have so appeared had it not much more
powerfully suggested one of the lower forms of organic life
monstrously enlarged to some problematical but assuredly
sinister end. Into the belly of this bug-like creature they
were presently bundled, but not before Mr. Thewless had
cast a final lingering look behind. He possessed, it is necessary to admit, something of an urban mind; and all too plainly
the entertaining little train spoke of a destination at the back
of beyond. Moreover, at this point of the journey there ceased
to be anything of that segregation of classes which the philosopher in him was accustomed to deplore but which the social
man was apt to take as part of the order of nature. Three or
four impoverished persons with bundles were already on
board, and immediately behind him an embarrassingly undernourished old woman was singing in a dismal, surprising and
Celtic manner—although whether for monetary reward or
the pleasures of self-expression was obscure. Presently the
driver appeared. He was a melancholy man lost in reverie—
and almost equally lost in an immensely old suit of Conne-
mara cloth, evidently tailored for one of the giants before the
Flood. He sat down before the controls, eyed them with that
flicker of interest which a person of abstract mind may evince
before some unfamiliar material thing, and presently pulled
a lever with every appearance of random experiment. The

bug instantly coughed violently, shuddered as if unkindly roused from sleep, gave a loud angry roar, and then abruptly fell silent and motionless once more. The driver again pulled the lever, but this time nothing happened at all. He tried several other controls with an equally negative result. Whereupon—but with the reluctance of one who is innately kindly —he reached for a large hammer, climbed down from his seat and proceeded to beat the bug violently about the snout. At this the bug, as if far advanced in some horrid masochistic perversion, contentedly purred. The driver climbed back into his seat and settled himself with an air of deep metaphysical abstraction. The bug continued to purr. After this nothing happened for quite a long time.

The bug purred and the August sun warmed both its entrails and that temporary ingestation represented by Mr. Thewless and his fellow travellers. Further impoverished persons crowded on board, the majority carrying ill-wrapped brown-paper parcels or uncertainly clothed children. Somebody brought up a number of cardboard boxes and proceeded to hoist them on the roof; these apparently contained young pigs and were rather smelly. Humphrey and Miss Liberty were discussing some nice point in the character portrayal of their author's middle period. The undernourished woman had stopped singing and was talking unintelligibly and uncomfortably down Mr. Thewless's neck. Probably she was soliciting alms. But as it was just possible that she was obligingly explaining some point of Hibernian scholarship germane to her minstrelsy he felt unable to take any action. Suddenly the purring deepened and the bug, without warning, shot off with a swaying and bouncing motion down the narrow-gauge line before it. At this the conductor, a fat boy with a squint who had been eating sandwiches at the back, showed much presence of mind by violently ringing a bell. Whereupon the driver, emerging in some degree from his

abstract speculations, as also from his enveloping suit, looked
about him in some perplexity and experimentally pressed a
button. Immediately a siren whooped demoniacally in the
bowels of the bug and amid a series of bumps and bucketings
the creature made for the open country. Overhead the piglets
in their cardboard boxes squealed in justifiable alarm. The
undernourished woman continued to talk down Mr. Thewless's neck, but her tone had changed and was now quite
evidently one of imprecation against a monster of parsimony.
A number of people ate oranges and close to Mr. Thewless a
small boy announced what was evidently a most implacable
intention to be sick. Everywhere the greatest good-humour
prevailed. From a wayside hoarding Northern Ireland took
a Parthian shot at the unregenerate:

THEIR WORM DIETH NOT
AND THE FIRE IS NOT QUENCHED. . .

The bug moved on. . . . For a couple of hours it purred
and clanked from station to station, but these halts grew
gradually more indeterminate in character as the afternoon
advanced, and eventually it simply stopped whenever summoned to do so by agitated persons hurrying across an
adjoining field. Once when the single track upon which
it ran breasted a rise Mr. Thewless was startled to see an
identical bug rapidly advancing upon them in the middle
distance. The driver, also by chance observing this appearance, called to the conductor, and the two engaged for
some minutes in dispassionate conversation, bending curiously
over the controls of the vehicle and pointing now to one
lever and now to another. Meanwhile, the advancing bug
hurtled towards them. The conductor made some suggestion
which the driver upon consideration rejected; the conductor
reflected and then urged some further argument; the driver,
being plainly a man of open mind, agreed to give the sugges-

tion a trial and depressed some object with his foot; with an agonising jolt the bug came to a dead halt. Some ten yards away the second bug had done the same, and the two appeared to eye each other balefully, much like two fleas that have been taught to simulate pugilistic encounter. The drivers and conductors, however, climbing out to meet upon neutral ground, debated the situation in the friendliest spirit over cans of tea and a cigarette; eventually the oncoming bug was coaxed by its crew to back for half a mile into a siding which had been discovered by the enterprise of a reconnoitring conductor—whereupon the journey was resumed.

MICHAEL INNES

124. FAINTHEART IN A RAILWAY TRAIN

At nine in the morning there passed a church,
At ten there passed me by the sea,
At twelve a town of smoke and smirch,
At two a forest of oak and birch,
    And then, on a platform, she:

A radiant stranger, who saw not me.
I said, "Get out to her do I dare?"
But I kept my seat in my search for a plea,
And the wheels moved on. O could it but be
    That I had alighted there!

THOMAS HARDY

125. FROM A RAILWAY CARRIAGE

Faster than fairies, faster than witches,
Bridges and houses, hedges and ditches;

And charging along like troops in a battle,
All through the meadows the horses and cattle:
All of the sights of the hill and the plain
Fly as thick as driving rain;
And ever again, in the wink of an eye,
Painted stations whistle by.

Here is a child who clambers and scrambles,
All by himself and gathering brambles;
Here is a tramp who stands and gazes;
And there is the green for stringing the daisies!
Here is a cart run away in the road
Lumping along with man and load;
And here is a mill and there is a river:
Each a glimpse and gone for ever!

ROBERT LOUIS STEVENSON

126. NIGHT MAIL

This is the night mail crossing the border,
   Bringing the cheque and the postal order,
Letters for the rich. letters for the poor,
   The shop at the corner and the girl next door,
Pulling up Beattock, a steady climb—
   The gradient's against her but she's on time.

Past cotton grass and moorland boulder,
   Shovelling white steam over her shoulder,
Snorting noisily as she passes
   Silent miles of wind-bent grasses;
Birds turn their head as she approaches,
   Stare from the bushes at her blank-faced coaches;
Sheepdogs cannot turn her course
   They slumber on with paws across,

In the farm she passes no one wakes,
    But a jug in a bedroom gently shakes.

Dawn freshens, the climb is done.
    Down towards Glasgow she descends
Towards the steam tugs, yelping down the glade of cranes
    Towards the fields of apparatus, the furnaces
Set on the dark plain like gigantic chessmen.
    All Scotland waits for her;
In the dark glens, beside the pale-green sea lochs,
    Men long for news.

Letters of thanks, letters from banks,
    Letters of joy from the girl and boy,
Receipted bills and invitations
    To inspect new stock or visit relations,
And applications for situations,
    And timid lovers' declarations,
And gossip, gossip from all the nations,
    News circumstantial, news financial,
Letters with holiday snaps to enlarge in,
    Letters with faces scrawled in the margin,
Letters from uncles, cousins and aunts,
    Letters to Scotland from the South of France,
Letters of condolence to Highlands and Lowlands,
    Notes from overseas to the Hebrides;
Written on paper of every hue,
    The pink, the violet, the white and the blue,
The chatty, the catty, the boring, adoring,
    The cold and official and the heart's outpouring,
Clever, stupid, short and long,
    The typed and the printed and the spelt all wrong.

Thousands are still asleep
   Dreaming of terrifying monsters
Or a friendly tea beside the band at Cranston's or Crawford's;
   Asleep in working Glasgow, asleep in well-set Edinburgh,
Asleep in granite Aberdeen.
   They continue their dreams
But shall wake soon and long for letters.
   And none will hear the postman's knock
Without a quickening of the heart,
   For who can bear to feel himself forgotten?

W. H. AUDEN

127. THE AMHERST TRAIN

I like to see it lap the miles,
And lick the valleys up,
And stop to feed itself at tanks;
And then, prodigious, step

Around a pile of mountains,
And, supercilious, peer
In shanties by the sides of roads;
And then a quarry pare

To fit its sides, and crawl between,
Complaining all the while
In horrid, hooting stanza;
Then chase itself down hill

And neigh like Boanerges;
Then, punctual as a star,
Stop—docile and omnipotent—
At its own stable door.

EMILY DICKINSON

128. THE IRON STEED

In our black stable by the sea,
Five and twenty stalls you see—
Five and twenty strong are we:
The lanterns tossed the shadows round,
Live coals were scattered on the ground,
The swarthy ostlers echoing stept,
But silent all night long we slept.
Inactive we, steeds of the day,
The shakers of the mountains, lay.
Earth's oldest veins our dam and sire,
Iron chimeras fed with fire.
All we, the unweary, lay at rest;
The sleepless lamp burned on our crest;
And in the darkness far and nigh,
We heard our iron compeers cry:

Soon as the day began to spring. . .

ROBERT LOUIS STEVENSON

129. THE EXPRESS

After the first powerful plain manifesto
The black statement of pistons, without more fuss
But gliding like a queen, she leaves the station.
Without bowing and with restrained unconcern
She passes the houses which humbly crowd outside,
The gasworks and at last the heavy page
Of death, printed by gravestones in the cemetery.
Beyond the town there lies the open country
Where, gathering speed, she acquires mystery,
The luminous self-possession of ships on ocean.
It is now she begins to sing—at first quite low
Then loud, and at last with a jazzy madness—

The song of her whistle screaming at curves,
Of deafening tunnels, brakes, innumerable bolts.
And always light, aerial, underneath
Goes the elate metre of her wheels.
Steaming through metal landscape on her lines
She plunges new eras of wild happiness
Where speed throws up strange shapes, broad curves
And parallels clean like the steel of guns.
At last, further than Edinburgh or Rome,
Beyond the crest of the world, she reaches night
Where only a low streamline brightness
Of phosphorus on the tossing hills is white.
Ah, like a comet through flame, she moves entranced
Wrapt in her music no bird song, no, nor bough
Breaking with honey buds, shall ever equal.

                                        STEPHEN SPENDER

130. SUNDAY ON A BRANCH LINE

THE guard blew his whistle and waved his flag—how
weighted with ritual have the railways in their brief century
become!—and the train crawled from the little station. The
guard walked alongside through the snowflakes, wistful for
that jump-and-swing at an accelerating van that is the very core
of the mystery of guarding trains. But the train continued
to crawl. Sundry footballers in a glass box, some with legs
swung high in air, stood immobile to watch its departure.

The engine tooted. In pinnacled and convoluted automatic
machines, memorials of an age wildly prodigal of cast-iron,
the slowly moving traveller would have found it possible to
remark that the final and unremunerative penny had long
since been dropped. Long ago had some fortunate child
secured the last brightly wrapped wafer of chocolate; long
ago had the last wax vesta released a dubious fragrance from

the last cigarette—and the once flamboyant weighing machine, pathetic in its antique inability either to bellow or print, seemed yet, in its forlorn proposal to register a burden of thirty stone, whispering dumbly of dealings with a race of giants before the Flood.

Just such a well-cadenced if vacuous meditation as this might the passenger, drear and bored, have constructed for himself before the guard stepped resignedly aboard, the platform dipped, points sluggishly clanked and the train was in open country once more. Sunday afternoon, which in England subtly spreads itself over the face even of inanimate Nature, stretched to the flat horizon. The fields were clothed in patchy white like half-hearted penitents; here and there cattle stood steamy and dejected, burdened like their fellows in Thomas Hardy's poems with some intuitive low-down on essential despair; and now on the outskirts of a village the train trundled past a yellow brick conventicle constructed on the basis of hardly more cheery theological convictions. Inside the carriage it was cold and beginning to be fuggy as well. The focus of attention was a large glass bowl rather like those used in cemeteries to protect artificial flowers, but here pendulous from the roof and sheltering gas burners of a type judged moderately progressive at the Great Exhibition of 1851. Flanking this were luggage racks of a breadth nicely calculated to cause chronic anxiety in those below. Then came photographs: a beach and promenade densely packed with holiday-makers dressed in heavy mourning: a vast railway hotel standing, Chirico-like, in a mysteriously dispopulated public square: a grove exaggeratedly bosky and vernal, bespattered with tea tables and animated by three stiffly-ranked dryads in the disguise of waitresses.

Under the photographs were the passengers. Over the faces of the passengers, or lying on their knees, or slipped to their feet, were the objects of Sabbath devotion traditional

to Englishmen in the lower and middle ranks of society.
There were instruments and blunt instruments, packets of
weed-killer and bundles of incriminating letters. There were
love nests. There were park benches over which white
crosses and black circles hung mysteriously in air. There
were serious offences and grave charges; there were faces,
blurry and odd-angled, of judges, coroners, and detective-
inspectors from Scotland Yard. Thin-lipped and driven
women stood between policemen outside assize halls; persons
now of notorious life lay naked on horse-hair sofas waving
rattles, or dangled booted legs over Edwardian tables.

MICHAEL INNES

131. RAILWAY NOTE

The station roofs curve off and line is lost
In white thick vapour. A smooth marble sun
Hangs there. It is the sun. An ermine frost
Edges each thorn and willow skeleton
Beyond the ghosts of goods-yard engines. Who
On earth will get the big expresses through?
But these men do.
We ride incredulous at the use and eyes
That pierce this blankness: like a sword-fish flies
The train with other trains ahead, behind,
Signalled with detonation, whistle, shout;
At the great junction stops.
Ticket-collectors board us and fling out
Their pleasantry as though
They liked things so,
Answering the talkative considerate kind,
"Not so bad now, but it's *been* bad you know."

EDMUND BLUNDEN

The Grand Old Days

132. "YOU MUST TAKE YOUR TURN, MA'AM"

To Thomas Carlyle, Chelsea.

Templand, Saturday, July 19th, 1836.

ON Tuesday afternoon I reached Liverpool after a flight (for it can be called nothing else) of thirty-four miles within an hour and a quarter. I was dreadfully frightened before the train started; in the nervous weak state I was in, it seemed to me certain that I should faint, and the impossibility of getting the horrid thing stopt. But I felt no difference between the motion of the steam carriage and that in which I had come from London, it did not seem to be going any faster. As I had sent no intimation to Maryland Street, I was left to my own shifts on landing; the greatest difficulty was in getting my trunk from among the hundred others where it was tumbled. "You must take your turn, Ma'am, you must take your turn" was all the satisfaction I could get in pressing toward the heap; at last I said, "stand out of the road, will you? there is the trunk before my eyes; and I will lift it away myself without troubling anyone!" Whereupon the clerk cried out in a rage, "For Godsake give that Lady her trunk and let us be rid of her." The omnibus man clutched it out of my hands, and promised to put me down within ten yards of Maryland Street. He was better than his word, he drove me to the very door.

JANE WELSH CARLYLE

133. SEEING MR. SPENCER OFF

To see Mr. Spencer off on his travels from one of the large London stations was an experience not easily forgotten.

That fell to the lot of one of us in a year when his secretary happened to be away for his holiday.

First of all there was the great man himself to be looked after. Then his carriage in charge of his staid and solemn coachman. Then his carrying chair, his hammock, his rugs, air cushions, and endless small paraphernalia, the most important of which was the MS. of *Beneficence*—we think it was—which he carried himself, and for which he made a most amusing arrangement to insure its complete safety.

He tied a thick piece of string round his waist, which could not be seen—one end, however, was left two or three yards long, and this issued like a tail from underneath the back of his coat, and to its end the MS. was attached, made into a brown-paper parcel, which he then easily held in his hand. It so comically reminded us of the dog in the story-book which ran away with a saucepan tied to his tail that it sent us off into a peal of laughter. On learning the reason of our amusement he very soon joined in; all the same, he still continued to carry it in that droll way. The safety of the packet was of all importance, so appearances, as usual, mattered less than nothing at all.

On reaching the station he sat reading in the waiting-room while his "keeper" went to make various arrangements for the journey.

The railway officials were quite aggressive in their attentions, and continually inquired—

"Would Mr. Herbert Spencer like this?"

"Will Mr. Herbert Spencer have that?"

And finally—

"Will Mr. Herbert Spencer have our invalid chair to bring him from the waiting-room to the train?"

While declining that kind offer, it was impossible to disguise the amusement such a question occasioned.

The reason, however, soon became clear—for that was one of his best days—as an alert, upright man, with a healthy colour in his cheeks, walked with a swinging step rapidly along the platform, and quickly entered the saloon carriage which had been previously reserved.

Experience had taught him that by travelling in a hammock when going a long journey he avoided the evil consequences which usually followed the shaking of the train.

On that occasion he became so absorbed in superintending the slinging of it, that he did not at once observe the numerous inquisitive faces which peered eagerly through the windows at him.

Directly, however, he became conscious of them, out rang in stentorian tones to the porters—

"Draw down those blinds!"

The four men present instantly sprang to do his bidding so the little entertainment for those inquisitive persons came to a sudden end.

When all was complete the officials were dismissed, and he climbed with some difficulty into his exceedingly unstable resting-place.

He settled down comfortably, and as the train was about

to start he warmly shook his companion's hand and delighted her by exclaiming—

"You have done very well! Good-bye."

ANON

134. TRAINS OF STATE

HER Majesty is not fastidious with regard to her travelling coaches. She does not travel in a train of such luxury as the late French Emperor, whose express consisted of nine richly appointed carriages and included a wine cellar and a conservatory of rare flowers. The Czar eclipses her Majesty in the sumptuousness of his railway travelling. He bought Napoleon's train, soon after the Emperor's capitulation at Sedan, adapted it to run on any gauge, enlarged it to fifteen saloons, and fitted it up as a sort of mansion on wheels, with every requisite according to a Russian's idea of home, perhaps the most lovely apartment in it being the Czarina's boudoir. Though the Queen's reign has been long and popular, and the gifts to her from all lands have been innumerable, no one seems to have thought of presenting her Majesty with a train.

She is less fortunate in this respect than the Emperor Francis Joseph, who, on June 2, 1891, inspected a handsome special train presented to him by the administrations of all the Austrian railways. The train, built at Prague at a cost of one hundred thousand florins, consists of eight vehicles. The imperial car, which runs the third from the engine, contains a sitting-room and bedroom beautifully panelled, and the ceiling, instead of being upholstered in silk, like the Queen's saloon, bears a pretty picture painted on the wood by an artist of Prague. In this car, which is flooded with light, so large are its plate-glass windows, there is also a toilet and bath-room, a special room for the Emperor's aide-de-camp, and a small room for his henchman. The fourth car contains a sitting-room and a number of bedrooms for the suite, and the fifth car a dining-room to seat sixteen persons, and a smoking-room; the after-part of the train being made up of a reserve car for a larger suite, a coach which is practically the kitchen, and a car for the servants and luggage. The wearer of the eagle and crown is greatly pleased with his palace on wheels, especially as it is well-appointed, not lacking in anything; and he can if he chooses, on any line in his realm, imitate the volatile legerdemain of the German Emperor, who, on his visit to this country in 1891, entered the special train at the Great Western station at Windsor in a tweed suit—"for once out of uniform and dressed like a private gentleman"—and alighted from the carriage, on the arrival of the train at Paddington, attired in the "striking uniform of the Queen's Dragoons"; making a quick change that would have done credit to Henry Irving in his character in the *Lyons Mail*, or to Teufelsdröckh himself, with all his knowledge of clothes, but was certainly bewildering to unimaginative people, who wondered how his Majesty had managed to leap out of the plain, unobtrusive garb of a civilian into a British officer's uniform.

JOHN PENDLETON

135. COIFFEUR'S SPECIAL

MR. ISIDORE, the Queen's coiffeur, who receives £2,000 a year for dressing Her Majesty's hair twice a day, had gone to London in the morning to return to Windsor in time for her toilet; but on arriving at the station he was just five minutes too late, and saw the train depart without him. His horror was great, as he knew that his want of punctuality would deprive him of his place, as no train would start for the next two hours. The only resource was to order a special train, for which he was obliged to pay £18; but the establishment

feeling the importance of his business, ordered extra steam to
be put on, and conveyed the anxious hair-dresser 18 miles in
18 minutes, which extricated him from all his difficulties.

THOMAS RAIKES

136. THE EASTERN COUNTIES

EVEN a journey on the Eastern Counties must have an end
at last.

WILLIAM MAKEPEACE THACKERAY

WE do not really know what to do with this unnatural
corporation. They are hard at it again. From Shoreditch to
Yarmouth their whole line is a scene of that wild merriment
and frantic adventure conventionally characteristic of a
rover's cabin. Cambridge trains go to Hertford, and Hertford trains go off, and are never heard of again. We do
predict with the utmost confidence that there will in a few
years be a veritable county tradition of some lost Parliamentary train plying about Ely and Brandon, like the Flying
Dutchman round the Cape, with phantom stokers and ghostly
passengers, and perhaps a director on the tender condemned
in popular legends to a doom like that of the Wild Huntsman
of Saxony. Our paper last week conveyed almost daily
notifications of catastrophes or delays, and on Thursday we
were obliged to condense into a pregnant paragraph the
multitudinous mishaps that had occurred since the last
announcement. Happily, no great damage has lately fallen
on life or limb, but the worst results to the social and moral
condition of the people are impending. . . . East Anglia is
demoralized. A sentiment analogous to that most fatal effect
of servitude which makes the slave hug his fetters is rapidly
developing itself throughout this devoted district. Men
declare they *like* travelling on the railway. They snatch a

fearful joy from the romantic and hazardous character of the expedition, and would regard it as a spiritless and unstimulating incident if they were taken to the right station, with entire limbs, and in proper time. That yearning of Byron's hero for—

> ". . . all that gave
> Promise of pleasure, peril of a grave,"

is transferred to the hitherto sober and secluded peasant of the fens, and a spirit more reckless than that engendered by art unions is roaring and ramping over the sandy warrens of Norfolk. This will never do. . . .

THE TIMES, Saturday, 17 October 1846

137. ENTERPRISE

For 6d. the Great Eastern will deliver a large can of seawater at any address in London, calling next day to fetch the empty can without extra charge.

W. M. ACWORTH

138. THE NORTH BRITISH

Here is the company whose handling of expresses sheds anything but lustre on the Scottish nation. On the platforms of the Waverley station at Edinburgh may be witnessed every evening in summer a scene of confusion so chaotic that a sober description of it is incredible to those who have not themselves survived it. Trains of caravan length come in portentously late from Perth, so that each is mistaken for its successor; these have to be broken up and re-made on insufficient sidings, while bewildered crowds of tourists sway up and down amongst equally bewildered porters on the narrow village platform reserved for these most important expresses; the higher officials stand lost in subtle thought, returning now and then to repeated inquiries some master-piece of reply couched in the cautious conditional, while the hands of the clock with a humorous air survey the abandoned sight, till at length, without any obvious reason and with sudden stealth, the shame-stricken driver hurries his packed passengers off into the dark.

E. FOXWELL AND T. C. FARRER

139. THE HIGHLAND

THE utter absence of discipline at important stations defies description or explanation. The arrival or departure of a through train seems to be the signal for a general paralysis of common sense amongst all the station staff, who, instead of organising themselves to grapple with the crowd, at once lose heads or temper, and stiffen into philosophic apathy, until Time, of whom they never weary, brings their trouble slowly to an end. Why should we embark in our orderly thousands at Euston to be re-embarked a rabble at Edinburgh, Perth, or Inverness?

E. FOXWELL AND T. C. FARRER

140. WHEN BRITISH TRAINS RACED

IN this country the most celebrated railway races were those to Scotland over half a century ago. A traveller from London to Scotland had then, as he still has today, a choice of three routes. There was the line from Euston through Rugby and Crewe and up the north-west of England to Carlisle. There was the line from King's Cross through Peterborough and York along the north-east coast to Newcastle and Berwick. The third route followed a middle course from St. Pancras. This route went past Sheffield and Leeds to Carlisle.

For a number of reasons it was slower than the other two. But the wise traveller who did not wish to be hustled or crowded, and who was capable of enjoying the scenery after Leeds—easily the finest to be seen from any railway train in England—would (and even now should) use St. Pancras. Today that line is largely reserved for goods trains and cattle trains. How silly to keep what is most beautiful for the unheeding eye of sheep and bullocks, and to herd human beings along the humdrum routes to the east and the west!

Those routes—the east and the west—took about the same time to Edinburgh. They were therefore ideal for racing. Ever since the east coast route opened in the eighteen-fifties there had been constant rivalry. But warfare, open and declared, first broke out in the summer of 1888. In those days it took about nine hours from London to Edinburgh by the east route and about ten by the west. The racing began at the end of July and lasted until the middle of August. A train from Euston along the west route made the journey in seven hours thirty-eight minutes. That was nearly two-and-a-half hours quicker than before racing began, and three-quarters of an hour quicker than you can get to Edinburgh by the Midday Scot in 1951. The east coast route won the race, and it was a superb performance, by doing the journey in seven hours twenty-six and three-quarter minutes. That was one-and-a-half hours' speed-up as a result of racing and ten minutes quicker than the Flying Scotsman in 1951. Honour satisfied, the railway companies agreed to a truce—seven and three-quarter hours for the east; eight hours for the west. But like many another truce it was uneasy. Seven years later hostilities began again—this time much more exciting because the race was run by night, and was fought out to Aberdeen—almost 140 miles further than the race in 1888.

The struggle began in the middle of July 1895, and here I should explain why these races took place in high summer.

The reason for this was that the railway companies were fighting to capture the sporting public going to Scotland for the grouse shooting. If it is not offensive to the memory of these long-dead sportsmen, I should say that they were the most valuable passenger traffic on the English railways—a prize really worth winning. They travelled with perhaps their wives—certainly a female companion—plenty of servants, dogs, guns and luggage. Above all, they paid their lavish way in golden sovereigns, and out of their own pockets. No modern nonsense about putting down the cost of their journey to expenses, on the ground that they were going to provide the Ministry of Food with grouse for the London restaurants. They were ideal railway passengers. They were not very politely known in official railway circles as "The Grouse Traffic."

The race of 1895 began so quietly that the public hardly realised what was happening. Of course, in those days there were no public relations officers. Our forebears realised that human beings are sometimes more impressed by what they find out for themselves than by what they are told by officials —which reminds me that the best people for unravelling facts about the railways have always been the clergy of the English Church: they are the watchdogs of our railway system. For this I offer no explanation, unless it be the attraction of opposites—the rush and bustle of the railways in contrast with the unruffled lives of those who adorn our rectories and vicarages. If I came across a nasty problem in a railway timetable I should always go to a clergyman for its solution. But the interest of the clergy in railways is not limited to timetables. The most graceful writer about railway trains today is a Canon of Winchester and the finest amateur photographer of railways is the Archdeacon of one of our great northern towns.

Therefore it was no surprise to me to discover that the first person to realise that the race was on in 1895 was a clergy-man. On Monday, July 15, this gentleman (no doubt enjoying a little relaxation after a strenuous Sunday) was strolling round Euston station. He was startled to see huge blue posters round the entrance which announced "The 8 P.M. from Euston will now reach Aberdeen at 7 A.M.—an acceleration of one hour." Now the clergyman knew what was what, and he bustled down the road to King's Cross. He arrived just in time to see a high official of that railway, resplendent in top hat and with the gleam of battle in his *pincenez*, boarding the train for York, where he was going to make arrangements for the east to answer the challenge from the west.

One of the difficulties in arranging these races was that the trains had to travel over the lines of several different companies. From Euston you ran as far as Carlisle on the London and North Western. From Carlisle you went to Aberdeen by the Caledonian Railway—an outstandingly lovely line with brilliant blue engines. The King's Cross route was more complicated. The Great Northern took you to York; there the North Eastern took over to Edinburgh, and from Edinburgh the North British took on to Aberdeen. Although the carriages ran right through from London to Aberdeen, each change of company meant a change of engine. The advantage to the west route of having only a single change of company at Carlisle was considerable. To make up for this the advantage of geography lay slightly with the east route.

A railway map will show you that after Carlisle and Newcastle the two routes to Aberdeen converge—gradually but quite perceptibly. They finally meet at a place called Kinnaber Junction—just beyond Montrose. From there they travel over the same line to Aberdeen. Whoever reached Kinnaber first had won the race. The man in the signal box at Kinnaber was a member of the Caledonian staff—a man whose sympathies were naturally with the west, and he had the crucial task of letting through the victor.

On July 22—that is, a week after the posters had appeared at Euston—the east coast route advertised that their train would reach Aberdeen at 6.45—a quarter of an hour before the west. Now the authorities at Euston were rather modern in their ideas of warfare. They believed in a fierce thrust without any declaration of war. They accordingly said nothing, but knocked twenty-five minutes off their time and slipped into Aberdeen at 6.35—ten minutes before the east coast train. A week later the east coast advertised that their train would arrive at 6.25. Again the west coast authorities maintained a sphinx-like silence, but timed their train five minutes earlier. In fact the west coast train steamed into Aberdeen on July 30 at a minute to six—that is ten hours for the trip of well over 500 miles.

The west coast had, during this period of the race, a huge advantage. They could control their stopping time all the way to Carlisle. Nothing holds back a train's time more than stops in which luggage vans have to be cleared, nervous passengers shepherded on and off the train. The west coast trains stopped only at Crewe between London and Carlisle. The staff at Crewe did a magnificent job in clearing the vans and pushing on the passengers like greased lightning. One evening a porter, shepherding an old lady into a comfortable seat, was carried off to Carlisle. If the train "made" time between London and Crewe, the stationmaster at Crewe got it away even if it was in advance of its time.

The east coast could not do this so easily because after York the other companies—that is the North Eastern and the North British—insisted on keeping to the timetable. The North British—with the respect for authority which is perhaps a characteristic of the Scot—were absolutely maddening. On one occasion they held the east coast express back for nine minutes in Waverley Station, Edinburgh. But by very tactful handling the authorities at King's Cross were eventually able to persuade these other companies to pay no attention to tiresome things like timetables. Consequently when this was done there was a tremendous race on the night of August 15. At Kinnaber the bell in the signal box rang to announce the arrival of the west train precisely one minute before it rang to announce the arrival of the east train. On the following night both bells rang together. The signalman—and it will be remembered that he was a west man, a Caledonian servant —gave the road to the rival company. A really fine example of the sporting spirit shown throughout, because it should not be overlooked that these races were a great strain not only on the drivers but on station and signal-box staff over both routes.

On the night of August 21 the east coast companies carried their train through in eight hours forty minutes. They were at Aberdeen at 4.40 A.M. The west coast train arrived fourteen-and-a-half minutes later. On the following night the west coast, with a train stripped for racing, did the journey in the astonishing time of eight hours thirty-two minutes. The race was over. Today the journey by either route now takes something in the neighbourhood of twelve hours. As we compare these times we might say with the great Roman of old: "Oh, what a fall was there, my countrymen!" I well know that railway authorities do not like to be reminded of these glories of other days. And to be fair, there are many good reasons why those speeds of 1895 were not economic and could not be maintained. But it was a superb achievement to travel that distance, well over 500 miles, at an overall speed of more than 60 m.p.h.

During the height of battle some sharp things were said. Supporters of the west complained that the sleeping-cars on the east were not heated and had no attendants. And they also complained that at Waverley Station, Edinburgh, where there was just time for a snack, the eggs were always stale. Supporters of the east coast replied with a dirty thrust. They said that the arrangements on the west route for the engine to take up water while travelling were dangerous and might cause an accident. This was dirty—really a blow below the belt, because the public were terribly easily frightened and, ever since the days of Dickens, had believed that high speeds were the cause of smashes. The railway authorities did their best to counter this by issuing a statement that a speed of 70 m.p.h. was not enough to spill a cup of coffee and they argued that this was due to gyrostatic action which explained why a bicycle is steadier when ridden fast. I suppose the Rotor at Battersea illustrates the same simple truth.

But not all the public was convinced. There were the health bores who argued that increased speed meant increased vibration which was most wearing. Every train to Aberdeen, they argued, should include long stops so that passengers could have time to wash, and stroll along the platform, thereby restoring their shattered nerves and saving themselves hours of suffering. A gentleman actually wrote to the papers as follows: "I had to travel in a racing train and I reached Aberdeen in 10 hours. The oscillation was so great that I felt sick. Two of my servants were sick. A friend of mine only saved himself from sickness by a dose of brandy." Happy the traveller who had such an excellent excuse for a glass of brandy.

Night after night large crowds collected at King's Cross and at Euston to cheer the racers on their journey, and at each stop they were similarly encouraged—even at Carlisle at one o'clock in the morning. But the curious thing was that the companies never publicly altered their timetables and never openly admitted that a race was in progress. At a meeting of the North Western shareholders the Chairman said: "There is no such thing as a race." He then added the cryptic comment: "But our Company will not be last in it."

No doubt it is easy to say that the race to the north was pointless. Certainly the travellers who arrived at Aberdeen at 5 o'clock in the morning, and then had to wait two hours for breakfast, were not always enthusiastic. Yet it was a fine and spectacular advertisement for British railways. In a single night we doubly smashed the record (held by the Americans with their train from New York to Buffalo) for the fastest train in the world. It was a superb advertisement for the small engines of those days, for the rolling stock and for the permanent way. Above all, it was a tribute to the endurance and steadiness of British railwaymen. The highest speed of these trains has been exceeded in the twentieth century, but to have maintained such speeds for that distance, with the equipment then available, was an achievement which will never be surpassed.

Recalling these triumphs, we can, I think, warmly endorse some words once used by John Bright: "Railways have rendered more services, and have received less gratitude than any other institution in the land."

ROGER FULFORD

141. THE IRON DUKE

IT is not often that a member of the English aristocracy shows a liking for the footplate of an engine and the smell of railway grease; yet the Duke of Sutherland, who was among his own people familiarly called "The Iron Duke," because of his interest in railways, had a fancy for both. Nay, it is possible that it was from his grace that the Shah of Persia, who was his guest on his first visit to this country, got the quaint notion that stations are merely "places at which trains stop to have their wheels greased." When he was young and handsome, as the Marquis of Stafford ... he had ridden with the brigade on the swaying engine to many a great fire in the city; he had gone down many a pit to help after an explosion; he had chatted with many an iron-worker on the hot rim of the furnace, and gone day by day to the bedside of an engine-driver who had been nearly scalded to death. The navvy is no great respecter of persons. When roused he would thrash an earl as readily as he would maul the village constable; but he had a real respect for the Duke of Sutherland. One "navigator," striking his pick into the bank, and raising his ungainly form to admire his Grace, who was going out of Dunrobin Station with his hand on the regulator, said to his mate ... "There, that's what I call a real dook! Why, there he is a-driving of his own engine on his own railroad, and a-burning of his own blessed coals!"

JOHN PENDLETON

142. THE RAILWAY SANDWICH

THERE could be no better breakfast than used to be given in the buffet at the railway terminus at St. Michael. The company might occasionally be led into errors about that question of coupé seats, but in reference to their provisions, they set an example which might be of great use to us here in England. It is probably the case that breakfasts for travellers are not so frequently needed here as they are on the Continent; but still, there is often to be found a crowd of people ready to eat if only the wherewithal were there. We are often told in our newspapers that England is disgraced by this and by that; by the unreadiness of our army, by the unfitness of our navy, by the irrationality of our laws, by the immobility of our prejudices, and what not; but the real disgrace of England is the railway sandwich,—that whited sepulchre, fair enough outside, but so meagre, poor, and spiritless within, such a thing of shreds and parings, with a dab of food, telling us that the poor bone whence it was scraped had been made utterly bare before it was sent into the kitchen for the soup pot. In France one does get food at the railway stations, and at St. Michael the breakfast was unexceptionable.

ANTHONY TROLLOPE

143. EVERLASTING COFFEE

A TRAIN on the South Eastern line stopped at Tunbridge station, and the passengers rushed out to obtain some refreshment. They had hardly begun to sip their hot coffee, when the bell rang, and the exclamation of the guard, "Now, gentlemen, take your places, if you please," compelled them, however reluctantly, to resume their seats. But, from some cause or other, the train did not start for several minutes, and before it left the station the travellers had the pleasure of seeing their almost brimming cups which they had left on the counter, emptied back into the urns for the next customers. As they rolled away, one of them made an estimate of how many times the same cup might thus be calculated to serve before it was finally consumed; but the result of this calculation, like many other theories, had better pass away without a record.

FREDERICK S. WILLIAMS

144. TO THE CATERER AT SWINDON

DEAR SIR,

I assure you Mr. Player was wrong in supposing that I thought you purchased inferior coffee. I thought I said to him that I was surprised you should buy such bad roasted corn. I did not believe you had such a thing as coffee in the place: I am certain that I never tasted any. I have long ceased to make complaints at Swindon—I avoid taking anything there when I can help it.

Yours faithfully,

I. K. BRUNEL

145. B.R. PLEASE COPY

No line has devoted so much attention as the Midland to its refreshment arrangements, which are, after all, though superior officers too often treat them as beneath their notice, by no means unimportant. Even the famous *buffet* at Avignon would hardly furnish a dinner of six courses and coffee for half-a-crown, as is done for Scotch passengers at Normanton; while the restaurant cars on the Continent certainly cannot surpass the dinners that are served in the Manchester and Leeds expresses. I should like, however, to suggest that some English railway might do worse than make trial of the German *transportable Speiseplatten*, or trays with legs, in place of luncheon baskets. "Non omnia possumus omnes"; and it is not given to every one to balance a mutton-chop and potatoes gracefully on his knee, the while he pours himself out a glass of claret with his hands.

But after all, though we may perhaps be in advance of the Western States, in which, according to the *Omaha World*, burglars have abandoned their profession and taken to railway restaurant-keeping as less dangerous and more lucrative, we in England cannot touch the completeness of the Indian arrangements. Here is a cutting from a recent Australian paper referring to the line from Calcutta to Bombay: "The refreshment-rooms at the several places along the line were very good. For *chota-hazri* (little breakfast), which we took just after daybreak, we would have a cup of tea and some toast or bread and butter. Breakfast proper followed this at 9 or 10 o'clock, then tiffin at 1, and dinner about 6 in the evening.

All the meals were exceptionally good. For dinner there would be, besides soup and fish, beef, mutton, snipe, duck, partridge, quail, pastry, four or five different kinds of fruits, and the universal curry and rice. The tables were laid more in the style of a first-class club than a railway refreshment-room; and there was a native servant to every two passengers who partook of meals. The guard or some other official of the train came to our carriage some fifty miles before we were to stop for tiffin or dinner and asked what wine or beer we wished to have, and he would then send a wire for it to be put in ice. The charges were for breakfast or tiffin about one shilling, and for dinner half-a-crown."

W. M. ACWORTH

146. THE OXFORD RAILWAY CLUB

OF all the clubs the Railway Club was the most original. This was founded by John Sutro in 1923. In addition to his rare gifts as guide, philosopher and friend to all my generation, a consummate actor, mimic, improviser, journalist, vocalist, pianist and gastronomist (it would take me too long to catalogue all his talents), John Sutro had a deeply personal affection for the British Railway Companies and a feeling for British trains and their affinities that was alternatively, lyrical, ethical, aesthetic, practical and patriotic. Stationmasters, stewards and railway porters beamed upon him, and this warm glow communicated itself even to the locomotive. To travel with him on any line was a novel experience, for the train realized it had a wooer on board: it slowed down when the scenery became interesting, gathered speed when it grew dull, and all the way it sang at the top of its lungs, never stinting itself, and giving of its best.

Fellow passengers turned into cousins or trusted family friends, chatting and relapsing into silence in response to one's moods. John Sutro himself was as radiant as Father Christmas, the incarnation of human benevolence. Each railway journey was packed with incident. I could never quite grasp how it happened. Telegrams were dispatched and trunk-calls put through at the stations *en route*, which wore a festive air. In the station restaurants, one was surprised to find lobsters, dressed crabs and other dainties, as fresh as if they had just come out of the sea. Wherever one went, John wrought this miracle. He loved the British trains and they loved him. And this mutual love gave birth to delightful and unexpected situations. Of course he knew the time-tables by heart. He could tell you where to change and how to employ your time to best advantage between different connexions.

The organization of a Railway Club at Oxford was no light matter, for John did everything on a grand scale, and we were to celebrate with a banquet on the railway once a term. Since we had to be in college by midnight our time on the train was curtailed. Our inaugural journey took us to Leicester and back. A saloon was reserved on the Aberdeen–Penzance Express to accommodate members and guests, some sixteen altogether. We devoured a substantial dinner, superior to the usual fare in railway restaurants. The chef had evidently taken a special interest in its preparation, and it was served on spotless napery. Wine lent a Horatian charm to the scenery, and the train serenaded us as we discussed the developments of travel since Stephenson's "Rocket." With the coming of railways a new sense of speed had entered the world, and in this respect also Early Victorian England was comparable with the England of To-day. Witness Turner's "Rain, Steam and Speed."

All too soon we arrived at Leicester, where the station bar received us with open arms. For twenty minutes we sipped rare liqueurs, Grand Marnier and green Chartreuse now long extinct, in that hospitable atmosphere. The return journey was devoted to oratory. The excellence of the dinner, the genial rhythm of the train, combined to promote fine flights of eloquence. We toasted his reigning Majesty, his late, more congenial Majesty Edward the Seventh, the British Railway Companies, the Steward of the train and a galaxy of others. I delivered a speech in praise of "Fantastica," whose health was drunk amid riotous applause. It was the forerunner of many witty evenings, each with a unique flavour. On another occasion we took a saloon to the railway junction of Bletchley in combination with the Cambridge Railway Club. But a 'flu epidemic had decimated the latter, whose aims, it appeared, were different from ours. Our journeys became longer and more adventurous, culminating in a stupendous visit to Brighton, where we were entertained by Sir Harry Preston at the Royal Albion Hotel with Edwardian splendour. So loath were the members to forsake a noble tradition that our meetings continued long after we had graduated, until 1939.

HAROLD ACTON

147. A HAVEN OF REFUGE

WHEN some rather fussy penitent told his father confessor that he could find nowhere in London where he could meditate in quiet and peace, he was astonished to hear the caustic answer, "Have you tried Marylebone station, my son?"

CANON ROGER LLOYD

148. SENTENCED TO BRADSHAW

WHEN Archbishop William Temple was Headmaster of Repton he used to sentence the wicked with an original form of imposition. He would produce a copy of Bradshaw's Railway Guide, and order the offender to find out the quickest and best way of travelling from, say, Great Yarmouth to Exeter, or Penrith to Ipswich, without touching London. The boy had to write down all the changes, and the times of arrival and departure at every point of change. When the imposition was shown-up, Temple would look at it with an expert eye, and would often tell him that he knew a better way of doing the journey. From memory, for he was almost as good at Bradshaw as he was at everything else, he would correct the boy's time-table and triumphantly arrive at Exeter or Ipswich an hour or more earlier than the boy's paper said he could.

CANON ROGER LLOYD

149. THE BLACKLEG

To this day I have little idea of what the General Strike was about; I was too young at the time to take much interest in its political causes and now I am twice as old the whole thing is rather stale. As one who has since joined a Trade Union I am usually rather reticent in referring to my activities during the Strike; I fear they might be misunderstood and my principles questioned.

The truth is, of course, that I and some 2,000 other young men at Cambridge went to work in the General Strike with no thought of strike-breaking, of being "patriotic," saving the country from Bolshevism or anything like it. We saw in the whole business nothing more or less than a heaven-sent opportunity to run a railway.

To begin with I reported at six o'clock every morning dressed in a blazer and plus-fours and worked as a porter; my picture was taken and appeared as the personification of "The Lighter Side" in the local Press. I had a bottle of beer in my hand at the time, for we were generously supplied with quantities of free drink and food. I did not greatly relish moving boxes of ageing fish, so I ceased to be a porter after a day or so and became a guard.

I was lectured on a guard's duties and responsibilities by an old retired railwayman, given a whistle, red and green flags, a handful of fog detonators and told to report for the 6.30 A.M. to Ely the following morning.

When I arrived at the train I found that I was by no means the only guard in the van. There were sixteen others, each of whom had been instructed to report at the same time and place. Our train consisted of two or three coaches and was driven by an engine-driver and a stoker who were rowing Blues. During our maiden voyage the stoker unwisely stood up on the tender as we went under a bridge; but he came back next day, with his head bandaged and helped us to keep our record of having the only engine on the line that didn't go off the boil.

Our main job on a round trip to Ely and back was to collect the milk. At the first stop I understood why seventeen guards were considered necessary. I approached a churn on the platform and prepared to roll it in the casual manner I had seen porters employ. We needed every one of seventeen guards to collect the milk; the churns which are rolled so easily are the empties. Full churns weigh like lead.

The Ely milk train carried no passengers even though accommodation was provided for them and the train's schedule was advertised in the Press. We used our flags and whistles, even the fog signals were exploded on the line to hear what kind of noise they made; but none of us ever punched a ticket.

At last, one morning as we drew into a country station we saw two elderly women standing on the platform waiting for the train. Our engine driver overshot the station by fifty yards in his excitement and if a public-spirited small boy had not previously opened them we would have shattered the level-crossing gates ahead of us. When the train had been manœuvred into position, seventeen guards scrambled out with ticket-punches in hand to show our first passengers into the best first-class seats (nobody had provided us with forms for excess fares, so we couldn't have taken any extra money if we'd wanted to).

All our invitations were refused. Imagining that perhaps the two women had been unable to buy tickets and were shy of boarding a train without paying, we assured them that they could pay the other end. We were still anxious to have passengers even if they had no tickets for us to punch.

We asked the women where they wanted to get to.

"Oh," replied one of them sweetly, "we're not travelling anywhere. We've just come to say how *wonderful* we think you boys are!"

It was a dejected whistle which gave the right-away to the driver, and on the return journey our van echoed to coarse and bitter words on the subject of public ingratitude. On my return to Cambridge I gave up being a guard and became a signalman, though not until I had worked as guard behind 52 trucks of rotting cabbages which had to be taken to Tottenham.

To the layman the guard of a goods train appears to have an easy life spent in brewing tea or toasting kippers over the stove in his van. In reality it is an energetic existence. British goods trains do not as a rule have Westinghouse brakes, so that when the train goes down hill you hear the clanking of buffers getting near you as the engine puts on its brakes. The guard then turns his own brake-wheel furiously and holds on for dear life as the full force of 52 trucks hits the brake-van a tremendous crack.

A signalman's life provides more opportunity for tea and kippers, though my first spell in a signal box during the Strike offered a little too much leisure. I had the misfortune to be posted to a box just outside Cambridge station, where I found a young viscount (now a Tory M.P.) already installed and resentful of the idea that he needed an assistant. He refused to allow anybody but himself to touch the signals, and after a few hours of inactivity, my mates and I (the authorities considered every job on the railway should be done in triplicate at least) bade his lordship a good day and left.

We were then sent to another box at the junction near Shelford, where one line goes from Cambridge to Liverpool Street, another to King's Cross and a third to some small market town in Suffolk.

We were much happier in this box. Every day at one o'clock the only passenger train of the day passed, bound for Liverpool Street, and the guard would throw our lunch and a bottle of beer on the grass verge as the train went by.

One day, though, the guard was careless; our lunch landed on the grass, but the beer bottle hit the side of the signal box and was broken.

The next day the 1 P.M. Up never got to Liverpool Street at all; or if it did, it wasn't the fault of anybody in our box, for we set the points so that the train went along the line to some unknown destination in Suffolk. And for all we know or care, that train is still there.

Shortly afterwards the General Strike ended; we were all paid handsomely for many hours of overtime and I was a little disappointed when, drawing my money at the Labour Exchange, I was not allowed to have a card entitling me to draw the dole as an out-of-work railwayman. I have been told by strikers who were "out" during the General Strike that they felt they had lost something when it was all over. They were not the only ones; those few days in May, 1926, were, for thousands of us, pure, ecstatic wish-fulfilment.

SPIKE HUGHES

150. NIGHT SPECIAL FROM INVERNESS

LESS than three weeks after landing in Norway I found myself flying back to England, bearing dispatches of a most unhopeful kind to the C.I.G.S. The Allied Force Commander at Namsos was General Carton de Wiart, who has only one eye, only one arm, and—rather more surprisingly—only one Victoria Cross. Though not a man to be easily daunted, he found himself unable to share the comparative optimism with which London appeared to be regarding the situation, and having written his dispatch he ordered me to deliver it personally to the War Office and to be prepared to answer any questions which the people there might want to ask me.

Another Sunderland took me back across the North Sea to Invergordon, but bad weather made it impossible to land and we had to go all the way up to the Shetlands. Next morning the weather was still bad but I got into Invergordon in the afternoon and transferred to a bomber which was standing by to fly me to London. We took off; but the weather was getting worse again. After about an hour the pilot turned back and we landed once more at Invergordon.

I was now, as perhaps you can imagine, in a state of some impatience and anxiety. I knew the importance of the dispatches I carried. I knew they should have reached the War Office twenty-four hours ago. As it was, they were still 500 miles from Whitehall and the weather reports were gloomy. I decided to cut my losses and catch the night train from Inverness. This proved to be out of the question. It was a Saturday night, and the only train leaving Inverness for the south would have left before I could get there from Invergordon. I became, in a quiet sort of way, desperate. Hitler had missed the bus in Norway, I had missed the train at Inverness; but it did not seem to have made much difference to Hitler, and I determined that it should make as little to me. I rang up the stationmaster and ordered a special train. I would sign for it, and I felt sure the War Office would be delighted to pay. The stationmaster was a splendid man. Instead of asking a lot of silly questions he asked the only one that mattered: What time did I want to start? I said I should like to get some dinner first, and he said, Very well, he would have the train ready outside the station restaurant at half-past nine.

And there it was when the time came: an enormous railway engine, a sleeping-car, and one or perhaps two other coaches to keep it properly trimmed at high speeds. The sleeping-car was a special one, panelled with exotic timbers from different parts of the Empire; I think it had been in some kind of exhibition. It was a lovely train. And how pleasant to be able to say to various old friends that one met in the Station Hotel, "You don't happen to want a lift to London tonight, do you?" And when the three or four who accepted were on board, with how casual, how proprietary, how smug an air one glanced at one's wrist-watch and, leaning out of the window, said to a kindly railway official, "I'm ready to start, if your people are."

PETER FLEMING

Journey's End

151. TO A GREAT-WESTERN BROADGAUGE ENGINE AND ITS STOKER

So! I shall never see you more,
You mighty lord of railway-roar;
The splendid stroke of driving-wheel,
The burnished brass, the shining steel,
Triumphant pride of him who drives
From Paddington to far St. Ives.
Another year, and then your place
Knows you no more; a pigmy race
Usurps the glory of the road,
And trails along a lesser load.
Drive on then, engine, drive amain,
Wrap me, like love, yet once again
A follower in your fiery train.

Drive on! and driving, let me know
The golden West, its warmth, its glow.

Pass Thames with all his winding maze;
Sweet Clifton dreaming in a haze;
And, farther yet, pass Taunton Vale,
And Dawlish rocks, and Teignmouth sail,
And Totnes, where the dancing Dart
Comes seaward with a gladsome heart;
Then let me feel the wind blow free
From levels of the Cornish sea.

Drive on! let all your fiery soul,
Your puissant heart that scorns control,
Your burnished limbs of circling steel,
The throb, the pulse of driving-wheel,
O'erflood the breast of him whose gaze
Is set to watch your perilous ways.
Burn brighter in those eyes of vair,
Blow back the curly, close-cropped hair.
Ah! Western lad, would I might be
A partner in that ecstasy.

HORATIO F. BROWN

May 1891

152. THE SPIRITUAL RAILWAY

The line to heaven by Christ was made,
With heavenly truth the Rails are laid,
From Earth to Heaven the line extends
To Life Eternal where it ends.

Repentance is the Station then
Where Passengers are taken in,
No fee for them is there to pay
For Jesus is Himself the Way.

God's Word is the first Engineer
It points the way to Heaven so clear
Through tunnels dark and dreary here
It does the way to Glory steer.

God's love the Fire, His truth the Steam
Which drives the Engine and the Train
All you who would to glory ride
Must come to Christ, in Him abide.

In First and Second and Third Class
Repentance, Faith and Holiness
You must the way to Glory gain
Or you with Christ will not remain.

Come then poor sinners, now's the time
At any Station on the Line
If you'll repent and turn from sin,
The Train will stop and take you in.

FROM A TABLET IN ELY CATHEDRAL, 1845

153. AN ENGINE DRIVER'S EPITAPH

My engine is now cold and still,
No water does my boiler fill,
My coke affords its flame no more,
My days of usefulness are o'er;
My wheels deny their noted speed,
No more my guiding hand they heed;
My whistle—it has lost its tone,
Its shrill and thrilling sound is gone;
My valves are now thrown open wide,
My flanges all refuse to glide;

My clacks—alas! though once so strong,
Refuse their aid in the busy throng;
No more I feel each urging breath,
My steam is now condensed in death;
Life's railway o'er, each station past,
In death I'm stopped, and rest at last.

ANON

Notes

Kipling: From "The King" in *The Seven Seas*, 1896.

The Ringing Grooves of Change. Tennyson, *Locksley Hall.* He later annotated his technical mistake: "When I went by the first train from Liverpool to Manchester, I thought that the wheels ran in a groove. It was a black night and there was such a vast crowd at the station that we could not see the wheels." (Quoted in *Alfred Lord Tennyson: A Memoir,* by his son.)

3. *The Creevey Papers,* 1903–5.

4. *Records of a Girlhood,* 1878.

5. *Diary,* Vol. III.
Robinson became a devotee of railway travel. There are many references to his enjoyment of it in his letters to the Wordsworth, circle.

6. *Journal of the Reign of Queen Victoria,* First Series, 1874.

7. Quoted in Samuel Smiles, *Story of the Life of George Stephenson,* ed. of 1860.

8. *History of the English Railway,* 1851.
Subsequent passages by Francis are also from this book.

10. "Railway Morals and Railway Policy," *The Edinburgh Review,* 1854.

11. From a letter to I. K. Brunel's son; quoted by the latter in his *Life of I. K. Brunel,* 1870.

12. *Dombey and Son,* 1846.

13. *The Condition of the Working-class in England in 1844.*

14. *Story of the Life of George Stephenson,* 1857.

16. Quoted by G. M. Young in *Victorian England: Portrait of an Age,* 1936.

17. *Stokers and Pokers,* 1850.

18. *Circa* 1840.

19. From a letter to the King of the Belgians. *Letters of Queen Victoria*, Vol. I, 1907.

22. *Charlotte Bronte*, 1932.

23. *The Cestus of Aglaia*, 1865.

24. *Songs of the Rail*, 1878.
Anderson was a platelayer on the Glasgow and South-Western Railway.

26. *Studies of Sensation and Event*, 1843.

27. *Sermons in Sonnets*, 1851.

29. *The Railways of England*, 1889.
Subsequent passagse by Acworth are also from this book.

32. *The Setting Sun*, 1870.

33. In an article in *Leisure Hour*. The incident took place in the early 1840's.

34. *Journal*, Second Series, 1885.

36. *Monckton Milnes: The Years of Promise*, 1949.

37. E. Foxwell and T. C. Farrer, *Express Trains*, 1889.
Subsequent passages by Foxwell and Farrer are also from this book.

38. A Chinese Gentleman: *circa* 1875, when it was proposed to introduce railways into the Celestial Empire.

39. Scott: in a letter to Joanna Baillie, dated 18 July 1823.
Newman: *Apologia Pro Vita Sua*, Note A, ed. of 1886.

40. *Master Humphrey's Clock*, 1841.

41. *Selections from the Letters of Robert Southey*, 1856.

42. Ruskin: *Fors Clavigera*, Vol. I, 1871.
Arnold: *My Countrymen*, 1866.

43. Written on 12 October 1844.

44. *Letters of William and Dorothy Wordsworth*, Vol. III, The Later Years, ed. by E. de Selincourt, 1939.
The letter to the county members became two. They were published in *The Morning Post* on 16 October and 17 December 1844, and were subsequently reprinted at Kendal as a pamphlet.

45. *Lapsus Calami*, 1891.

47. From a letter to Cornell Price dated Avranche, Normandy, 10 August 1855. *Letters of William Morris*, ed. by Philip Henderson, 1950.

49. *An Account of the Liverpool and Manchester Rail-Way*, by Henry Booth, Esq., Treasurer to the Company. *Circa* 1832.

50. *Our Iron Roads*, 1852.
Subsequent passages by Williams are also from this book.

51. *Our Railways*, 1894.
Subsequent passages by Pendleton are also from this book.

52. From an Imperial Rescript of 17 March 1891.

53. Published by the Ministry of Communications, St. Petersburg, 1900. English translation by Miss L. Kukol-Yasnopolsky.

54. *Railway Problems in China*, New York, 1915.

55. Tarriers: Irish navvies, employed in large numbers on the construction of American railroads, especially in the 1880's.

57. *American Notes*, 1842.

58 & 59. Quoted in Joseph Husband, *The Story of the Pullman Car*, Chicago, 1917.

60. *Across the Plains*, 1892.
The Emigrant House was at the Pacific Transfer Station near Council Bluffs on the Missouri river.

61. *Autobiography of a Super-Tramp*, 1908.

63. "Huskisson, by nature uncouth and hesitating in his motions, had a peculiar aptitude for accident. He had dislocated his ankle in 1801, and was in consequence slightly lame. Twice he had broken his arm, and after the last fracture, in 1817, the use of it was permanently impaired.' *Dictionary of National Biography*.

64. *The Temple Anecdotes*, 1895.

65. From a letter quoted in Dionysius Lardner, *Railway Economy*, 1850.

68 & 69. *Old Euston*, 1938.

70. *Railroad Accidents*, New York, 1879.
Subsequent passages by Adams are also from this book.

72. *Engine-Driving Life or Stirring Adventures and Incidents in the Lives of Locomotive Engine-Drivers*, 1881.

75. *Letters of Charles Dickens*, ed. of 1893.
The smash occurred at Staplehurst, between Tonbridge and Ashford, on the South-Eastern Railway, 9 June 1865. Ten lives were lost.

77. There are many versions of the episode that gave rise to the

Casey Jones legend. According to one, Jones had replaced a sick friend on the footplate of the Illinois Central's crack express *The Cannonball*. The train was wrecked at Vaughan, Mississippi.

This syncopated version, and those of three other American folk-songs, Nos. 79, 81 and 83, were kindly supplied by Dr. Leslie Hotson, the Shakespearean scholar.

78. The accident occurred at Ashtabula, Ohio, 29 December 1876.

80. *The Octopus: A Story of California*, 1901.

84. McGonagall makes the bridge give way under the train. It is believed that, in fact, the wind carried away a section of the bridge beforehand, and that the train fell into the gap.

85. Translated from a news item in *Morgenbledet*, 20 February 1880 (about two months after the Tay Bridge disaster).

86. *Lapsus Calami*, 1891.

88. *The Fascination of Railways*, 1951.

Subsequent passages by Canon Lloyd are also from this book.

89. From "Railways, 1846" in *The Poetical Works of Charles Mackay*, 1876.

90. *Gryll Grange*, 1860.

91. *Dipsychus*, published posthumously, 1862.

92. From a letter dated Cambridge, Mass., 23 February 1853. *Prose Remains*, 1888.

93. From *Virginibus Puerisque*, 1881.

94. *Collected Poems*, 1947.

95. *Awake! and Other Poems*, 1941.

96. Greville: *Journal*, Second Series, 1885.

Bryant: *English Saga*, 1940.

98. *The Kaiser on Trial*, 1938.

99. *Seven Pillars of Wisdom*, 1926.

101. *The Listener*, 1 December 1949.

104. Letter to *The Times*.

106. *Fifty-five Years at Oxford*, 1945.

107. Published 25 March 1951.

109. Given at Liverpool by a Mr. A. J. Ellis. Quoted in Adams, *Railroad Accidents*.

110. Letter to John Ruskin. Quoted in *Præterita*, 1885–9.

111. *Collected Poems*, 1918.

112. *The Listener*, 6 March 1929.

113. *One's Company*, 1934.

114. *Letters of Eric Gill*, 1947.

115. *Return to Scotland*, 1930.
There is no difference in gauge between the Highland Railway and the other railways in the United Kingdom.

116. *The New Statesman and Nation*, 5 May 1951.

117. Lewis Carroll, *Through the Looking Glass*, 1871.

118. *Moments of Vision*, 1917.

119. *Collected Poems*, 1918.

120. *The Monomaniac* (*La Bête Humaine*). Translated by Edward Vizetelly, 1901.

121. *The Octopus: A Story of California*, 1901.

122. *Success*, 1902.
P. 203, lines 19–23.   From Penrith to Carlisle, Cunninghame Graham's train—which has been following the main West-coast route from Euston to Glasgow—is travelling on the wrong line. Little Salkeld, Armathwaite, Cotehill and Scotby are stations on the former Midland line from Appleby to the North. This runs some miles to the east of the main line to Scotland, and converges with it at Carlisle.

123. *The Journeying Boy*, 1949.

124. *Late Lyrics and Earlier*, 1922.

125. *A Child's Garden of Verses*, 1885.

126. Written for the film *Night Mail*, produced by the G.P.O. Film Unit, 1936. In the final sequence of the film the verse forms a recitative spoken by two voices, and is integrated with music by Benjamin Britten.

128. *Collected Poems*, 1950.
An unfinished fragment, probably inspired by Stevenson's journey across the States in 1879.

129. *Poems*, 1933

130. *Appleby's End*, 1945.

131. *Poems, 1914–1930*.

133. *Home Life with Herbert Spencer*, 1906.

135. *A Portion of the Journal kept by Thomas Raikes*, 1831–47.

140. *The Listener*, 2 August 1951.

141. The third Duke of Sutherland (1828–92) subscribed more than £250,000 to the building of railways, especially in Scotland. He was deeply interested in the technological development of the industrial revolution.

142. *He Knew He Was Right*, 1869.

146. *Memoirs of an Aesthete*, 1948.

149. *Opening Bars*, 1946.

150. *The Listener*, 24 November 1949.

151. *Drift*, 1900.

152. The tablet is to the memory of "William Pickering, Dec. 24, 1845, aged 30 years: Also Richard Edgar, who died Dec. 24, 1845, aged 24 years."

153. Inscription on a tombstone in the cemetery at Alton, Illinois.

The occupant of the grave was an engineer on the old Chicago and Mississippi Railroad. He was fatally injured in an accident, and is said to have written these lines while awaiting death.

Index of Authors Quoted

References are to page numbers and not to the numbers of items.